The Wall Street Hall of Fame
Biographical Portraits of the
Great Personalities in the
History of Business

Introduction

The history of America's economic growth is intimately tied to the events that marked the lives many of great men. The dynamic story of these famous personalities will be in capsule form so that they can all be included in one work.

They made America the richest and strongest nation in the world. Their urgent desire to span the plains with railroads, build the bridges, build the automobiles, drill for the needed petroleum, created new industries and millions of jobs. The fortunes that they accumulated were distributed among their heirs and in many cases were willed to foundations that remain today for worthy and philanthropic purposes.

The leadership and dynamism of these men should be an inspiration to every American. Their achievements are unique to the American way of life and remain so today. The fire which burned in the minds and hearts of these heroes, their quest for money, power, and status did not die with them. It lives on in the new generations that have followed.

D1530501

Preface

Over forty years ago I wrote an analytical bibliography that succinctly summarized the essence of 150 books on Wall Street. It was titled, "Best Books on the Stock Market." The American Library Association selected it as the best book of the year in finance.

I have a list of about 500 names under the title of "The Wall Street Hall of Fame. Many worthy individuals had to be denied entry because of the limited space. I have profiled almost 300 individuals. The 19th and 20th centuries witnessed the phenomenal growth of America. It led to the development of the leading economic juggernaut in the world. I think there is no way this could have happened without the effort of the personalities on this Hall of Fame. They had the ambition, energy, and audacity that it takes to succeed. Along with that success was money, power, and fame. Contrary to those who would claim that they couldn't do it alone, "they didn't build it"- I'm telling you, they did build it! And the success of America is the sum total of their individual accomplishments.

Therefore, I give you "The Wall Street Hall of Fame." It is the most comprehensive list of famous personalities who made America the leading economic power in the world. I wish to thank all those giants in the bibliography for the contribution they made, that allowed me to do this work. They deserve the credit for preserving the history of these men and women. Without their help, I would not have been able to create this historical work.

Table of contents
Members of the Hall of Fame

- Bronfman, Samuel
- Brown, Moses Henry
- Buffett, Warren Edward
- Busch, Adolphus
- Carlson, Chester Floyd
- Carnegie, Andrew
- Carrier, Willis Haviland
- Clark, William Andrews Sr.
- Clinton, DeWitt

- Colgate, William
- Colt, Samuel
- Cooke, Jay
- Cooper, Peter
- Cornell, Ezra
- Crocker, Charles
- Crown, Henry
- Cullman, Joseph Frederick III
- Curtis, Cyrus H. K.
- Curtiss, Glenn Hammond
- Danforth, William H.
- Davis, Arthur Vining "Art"
- Deere, John
- De Pew, Chauncey
- Disney, Walter Elias "Walt"
- Dorrance, John Thomas
- Dow, Charles Henry
- Drew, Daniel
- Dreyfus, Jack Jr.
- Duke, James Buchanan
- DuPont, Eleuthere Irenee
- Durant, William Crapo
- Eames, Francis L.

- Eastman, George
- .Eaton, Cyrus Stephen
- Eaton, Joseph Oriel II
- Edison, Thomas Alva
- Ellison, Lawrence Joseph "Larry"
- Evans, Oliver
- Fargo, William George
- Ferkauf, Eugene
- Field, Marshall
- Filene, William

Fisk, Jim Jr. (Jubilee)
- Flint, Charles R. Jr.
- Ford, Henry Sr.
- Franklin, Benjamin
- Frick, Henry Clay
- Fulton, Robert
- Gates, John Warne "Bet-a-Million"
- Gates, Bill (William Henry)
- Geneen, Harold Sydney "Hal"
- Getty, J. Paul "Jean"
- Gianinni, Amadeo Peter
- Gillette, King Camp
- Gimbel Brothers Inc.
- Gimbel, Isaac
- Girard, Stephen
- Goldman, Marcus
- Goldman, Sol
- Goodman, Henry
- Goodrich, Dr. Benjamin Franklin
- Goodyear, Charles
- Gould, Jay
- Grace, William Russell
- Graham, Benjamin (Grossbaum)

- Greeley, Horace
- Green, Hetty Robinson
- Greenberg, Maurice "Hank" Raymond
- Guggenheim, Isaac
- Guggenheim, Meyer
- Halliburton, Erle Palmer
- Hamilton, Alexander
- Hamilton, William Peter
- Hammer, Armand
- Hancock, John
- Harriman, Edward Henry "Ned"
- Hartford, George Huntington II
- Harvey, Fred Henry
- Hearst, George
- Hearst, William Randolph
- Hefner, Hugh
- Heinz, Henry John
- Hill, James Jerome
- Hollerith, Herman
- Hopkins, Johns
- Hopkins, Mark
- Hughes, Howard
- Hunt, H.L. (Haroldson Lafayette)
- Huntington, Collis
- Icahn, Carl
- Ingram, Billy and Anderson, Walter
- Insull, Samuel
- Jerome, Leonard W.
- Jobs, Steve
- Johnson, Robert Wood Jr.
- Jonsson, John Erik
- Kahn, Otto H. (Hermann)
- Keene, James R.

- Kaiser, Henry John
- Keep, Henry
- Kellogg, Will K.
- Kennedy, Joseph Patrick
- Kerkorian, Kirk
- Kettering, Charles F.
- Keynes, John Maynard
- Kluge, John Werner
- Knight, Phil
- Koch Family (Brothers)
- Kravis, Henry R.
- Kresge, Sebastian Spering (S.S.)
- Kroc, Ray Albert
- Kroger, Bernard Henry
- Land, Edwin H.
- Lauder, Estee
- Law, John
- Lazarus, Simon
- Lehman, House of
- Levitt, Arthur
- Levitt, William
- Lewisohn, Adolph
- Limbaugh, Rush
- Ling, James Joseph
- Livermore, Jesse L. (Lauriston)
- Loeb, Gerald M.
- Loeb, John Jr.
- Loeb, Solomon
- Loew, Marcus
- Longworth, Nicholas
- Lord & Taylor
- Lorillard, Pierre
- Love, James Spencer

- Ludwig, Daniel K.
- MacArthur, John Donald
- Mackey, John
- Macy, Rowland Hussey
- Magee, John
- Marcus, Bernie
- May, David
- McCormick, Cyrus
- McCullough, J.F. and Axene, Harry
- McCrory, John
- McDonald, Maurice and Richard
- Mellon, Andrew
- Mellon, Richard
- Monaghan, Tom
- Morgan, John Pierpont
- Morgan, Junius Spencer
- Morse, Samuel F.B.
- Murchison, Clinton Williams
- Nelson, Samuel A.
- Newhouse, Samuel Irving
- Nieman-Marcus
- Ohrbach, Nathan M.
- Olin, John Merrill
- Otis, Elisha Graves
- Packard, David
- Page, Larry
- Paley, William S.
- Peabody, George
- Penney, James Cash
- Perelman, Ronald Owen
- Pew, Joseph Newton
- Phipps, Henry Jr.
- Post, Charles W.

- Pulitzer, Joseph
- Pritzker, Jacob
- Pullman, George M.
- Raskob, John Jakob
- Redstone, Sumner Murray
- Rensselaer, Stephen Van
- Revson, Charles Haskel
- Richardson, Sid William
- Riklis, Meshulam
- Robber Barons, The
- Rockefeller, John Davison
- Rogers, Henry Huttleston
- Romney, Willard Mitt
- Rosenwald, Julius
- Rothschild, House of
- Rukeyser, Louis Richard "Lou"
- Russell, Richard
- Ryan, Thomas Fortune
- Sachs, Joseph
- Sage, Russell
- Sanders, Colonel Harland David
- Saunders, Clarence
- Schiff, Jacob
- Schultz, Howard
- Schwarzman, Stephen A.
- Sears, Richard
- Seligman, House of
- Seligman, Jesse
- Singer, Isaac Merrit
- Slater, Samuel
- Slim, Carlos
- Smith, Cyrus R.
- Smith, Fred

- Sobel, Robert
- Solomon, Haym
- Sperry, Elmer
- Spreckles, Claus
- Stanford, Leland
- Steinberg, Saul Philip
- Stewart, Alexander Turney
- Straus, Isidor
- Straus, Lazarus
- Strauss, Levi
- Swope, Gerard
- Taylor, Moses
- Thornton, Charles "Tex"
- Tiffany, Charles L.
- Tisch, Lawrence Alan
- Trippe, Juan Terry
- Trump, Donald John Sr.
- Tsai, Gerald
- Turner, Ted
- Untermyer, Samuel
- Vanderbilt, Cornelius "Commodore"
- Vanderbilt, William H.
- Vassar, Matthew
- Villard, Henry (Heinrich Hilgard)
- Walgreen, Charles
- Walton, Sam Moore
- Wanamaker, John
- Warburg, Felix
- Warburg, Paul
- Ward, Montgomery Aaron
- Washington, George
- Watson, Thomas John Sr.
- Weightman, William

- Weill, Sanford I. "Sandy"
- Wells, Henry
- Westinghouse, George Jr.
- Weyerhaeuser, Frederick
- Whitney, Eli
- Widener, Peter Arrell Brown
- Woolworth, Frank Winfield
- Wright, Orville
- Wright, Wilbur
- Wrigley, William Jr.
- Wynn, Stephen Alan (Steve)
- Zeckendorf, William Sr.
- Zuckerberg, Mark
- Zukor, Adolph

Author's Note

I owe a great debt of gratitude to all the many sources of biographical material, without which this book could not have been written.

All Americans should be aware of the contributions of the members of "The Wall Street Hall of Fame." Their ambition, their drive and audacity built America into the greatest economic power in the world.

The Wall Street Hall of Fame

Abraham, Abraham
1843-1911

Abraham Abraham was born in New York City in 1843, the son of Judah Abraham, who emigrated from Bavaria when he was fifteen. He was sent to the Bettlebeck & Company store in Newark, New Jersey to learn the dry-goods business. The other employees were Benjamin Altman and Lyman Bloomingdale, who were later to found their own department stores.

When he was twenty-two, Abraham opened a little dry-goods store on Fulton Street in Brooklyn. His partner was Joseph Wechsler. In 1893 Wechsler sold his half interest in the business to the three partners of Macy's, Isidor and Nathan Straus and Charles B. Webster. The name of the store was then changed to Abraham & Straus.

Abraham's death in 1911 was a great blow to Brooklyn, for which he had given so generously of effort, time, and money to local societies and institutions. His little shop had grown to a large department store employing 2,700 people and having annual sales of $13,000,000.

Adelson, Sheldon Gary
1933-

Sheldon Adelson is an American business magnate. He is chairman and chief executive officer of the Las Vegas Sands Corporation. The Sands is the parent company of The Venetian Macao Limited which operates The Venetian Resort Hotel Casino and The Sands Expo and Convention Center. Adelson also owns the Israeli newspaper Israel Hayom. He is the 12th wealthiest American. His personal wealth is estimated to be $20.5 billion as of September, 2012.

Adelson grew up in the Dorchester area of Boston, Massachusetts. His father was a taxi driver and his mother ran a knitting store. Adelson worked as a mortgage broker and an investment advisor and financial consultant. In the 1960s he sold toiletry kits and started a charter tours business. Adelson went to City College of New York, but dropped out. The original source of Adelson's wealth was the computer trade show Comdex, which he and his partners sold in 1995. Adelson's share of the $862 million was $500 million. In 1988, Adelson and his partners bought The Sands Hotel and Casino in Las Vegas. The next year they built the only privately owned convention center in the U.S.

In 1991, while honeymooning in Venice with his second wife Miriam, Adelson was inspired to build a mega resort hotel. He razed the Sands and spent $1.5 billion to construct The Venetian. The Venetian added a 1,013-suite tower, giving the hotel 4,049 suites, 18 restaurants, a shopping mall, etc.

In 2007, Adelson opened the $2.4 billion Venetian Macao Resort Hotel on Cotal. He planned to invest $1.2 billion and build on the Cotal strip by 2010 under the Four Seasons, St. Regis, and Sheraton brands. The one million square foot Sands Macao, was China's first Las Vegas-Style casino when it opened in 2004. Adelson recovered his $265 million investment in one year. He owns 69 percent of the stock. Since the opening of the Sands Macao, Adelson has increased his personal wealth more than 4 times. In Singapore, Adelson opened The Mandalay Sands for $5.5 billion. It has a shopping mall, a convention center, and 2,500 luxury hotel rooms.

During the 2012 presidential campaign, Adelson donated more than $50 million to Republican candidates. He has given many millions to various charities through his Adelson Foundation.

Allen, Solomon and Moses

The first major dealer in lottery tickets of all sorts were S. and M. Allen Company of Albany, New York, sons of an itinerant preacher in upstate New York. Solomon was a printer and saw the potential of lottery tickets. Lotteries were very popular when The Bank of the United States closed in 1812. A speculative fever spread across the country and the lottery business boomed. The Allens opened thirteen offices along the east coast from Boston to Mobile. They bought and sold tickets to the public and for their own account. Their success proved that distribution is the key to survival in the securities business. Their company ran into trouble after the closing of the Second Bank of the United States in 1832, and the depression that followed caused their creditors to force the liquidation of their company.

Their example paved the way for many more successful securities firms in the future. The Allens developed one of the first branch networks for selling paper assets to the public.

Armour, Philip
1832-1901

Philip Armour returned from the California gold fields to set himself up as a wholesale butcher in Chicago. He supplied the Union Armies with a great deal of pork. Armour and the pork-dealer Nelson Morris headed the two leading houses, along with fifty-four others who handled 900,000 hogs a year by 1865.

It was Armour who consummated one of the most famous business "coups" of the period. In 1865, Armour saw Grant's armies move on Richmond, and he was certain that the north would be victorious. He rushed to New York, sold quantities of pork short at $40 a barrel. After Appamatox, the commodity markets crashed. It ruined hundreds of traders, but it permitted Armour to cover his shorts at $18 a barrel. Overnight he gained $2,000,000 in quick profits. With this capital he increased his meat business, buying out his weaker competitors and improving his plant until it became one of the most prosperous industries in America.

Arison, Mickey
1949-

Mickey Arison is the chief executive officer of Carnival Corporation, the world's largest cruise operator, and owner of the NBA's Miami Heat.

Mickey is the son of the late Ted Arison, co-founder of Carnival with Meshulam Riklis. He lives in Bal Harbor, Florida, but has homes in New York, and Israel. He attended The University of Miami, but dropped out.

Ted Arison purchased Carnival for $1 when it had only one ship. Mickey Arison has almost $6 billion in assets by Forbes, and Carnival has about 100 ships. The major cruise lines that Carnival owns include Princess, Cunard, Costa, Holland America, and Seabourn.

Astor, John Jacob
1763-1848

John Jacob Astor was born in Waldorf, in the German Rhine country. At seventeen he set off for London. He learned about the fur trade from a furrier on the voyage to the United States. He went to work for a furrier in 1785. He married Sarah Todd, a sea captain's daughter, and opened a shop in his mother-in-law's home.

Astor soon got into New York real estate, buying up a long-term lease from Trinity Church for valuable land in what is now Greenwich Village. He lived at 221 Broadway and he acquired the lease from his next door neighbor, Aaron Burr, when he had to flee, after he shot Alexander Hamilton in a duel in 1804.

Astor built ships to carry furs to China and bring cargo back to America. He started the American Fur Co. He had nine ships and monopolized the fur business. He abandoned the business which he thought had a limited future and turned his attention to real estate, the spring that fed the greater part of his fortune. Astor amassed a total of $20 million.

Baker, George F.
1840-1931

George F. Baker built The First National Bank into the most powerful bank of its time, perhaps any time. Baker was born in Troy, New York. In 1813 he founded The First National Bank. He was a tough, silent leader who kept to himself in business and his personal life.

Congress investigated the "money trust." The hearings concluded that four men—Baker, Morgan, James Stillman, and John D. Rockefeller-held 341 directorships and controlled 112 companies with assets of $22 billion.

Baker was very charitable. He donated millions to charities and universities. Harvard buildings bear his name. His wealth was $200 million before the crash in 1929. He had three children. One of his sons Grenville, died of gunshot wounds in Florida in 1949, and a second son George F. III committed suicide 28 years later in 1977.

Baruch, Bernard Mannes
1870- 1965

Bernard M. Baruch is one of the most remarkable men in America's financial history. He was a contemporary of some of the legendary men during Wall Street's wildest and most exciting years. He had relationships with J.P. Morgan, Edward Harriman, "Diamond Jim" Brady, and "Bet-a-Million" Gates, and knew of the part they played in the skyrocketing finances of that era.

Baruch grew up in South Carolina. At the age of nineteen he was an office boy. Before he was thirty-five he was a millionaire. In the next fifty years Baruch grew to be a trusted advisor and counselor of presidents. He was a statesman who worked with two political parties and won the respect of both. Bernard Baruch was truly a distinguished American.

Bernard Baruch commented about "the age of excess" that culminated in the 1929 crash. He said, "When beggars and shoeshine boys, barbers and beauticians can tell you how to get rich it is time to remind yourself that there is no more dangerous illusion than the belief that you can get something for nothing."

Bell, Alexander Graham
1847-1922

Alexander Graham Bell was born in Edinburgh in 1847. His father and grandfather had done acoustical research. Bell had an intimate knowledge of their work. He was hired to teach two deaf mute girls in Boston. The parents of the girls backed Bell's experiments aimed at developing a harmonic telegraph. When his backers learned that Elisha Gray was working on the same principle, they dropped their support. Bell dropped this project and aimed at the more exciting one of trying to send audio voice over an electric wire.

One day Bell's associate Thomas A. Watson accidentally plucked a piece of clock wire, and Bell in another room, heard the twang, carried over a telegraph line. Finally, on March 10, 1876, Bell picked up his instrument and said, "Mr. Watson, come here, I want you," and Watson, holding the receiver in a distant room, heard the message. Bell had filed his patent application almost a month earlier, two hours before Elisha Gray filed his description based on the same principles.

History was made. The American Bell Telephone Company was organized in 1881. By 1900 American Telephone and Telegraph had taken over the business, there were 600,000 subscribers, and the company was growing faster than ever.

Belmont, August
1813-1890

August Schonberg was the son of a poor merchant in the Rhineland Palatinate in Western Germany. He was a wild, unruly, and undisciplined boy with a harsh tongue, who flouted his father's authority. He had a razor-sharp mind and a biting wit. He wanted to make money. At thirteen he went to Frankfurt and worked as an unpaid apprentice for the Rothschild's. One thing quickly became apparent to the Rothschild's—he was a financial genius.

August was transferred to Naples at the age of twenty-one, and then to Havana. When he heard of The Panic of 1837 in New York, he left Havana and with the Rothschild money, he began buying in a depressed market. A change then took place. His name became August Belmont and he was no longer a Jew or a German. "Some sort of Frenchman—we think." Thanks to the reservoir of the Rothschild's reserves, Belmont was able to start out in America, operating his own Federal Reserve System. He became a friend of bankers and the United States Government.

August Belmont became a figure At New York parties, both as a host and a guest. He spoke three languages-Italian, Spanish, and French. He was not handsome, he was short and stout. There was something about him that was hard to define. It was whispered that he had an insatiable appetite, and was a cruel and demanding lover.

Why was Belmont sent out of Europe by the Rothschild's? Why was the new bank not called N.M. Rothschild & Sons, rather than August Belmont & Company? The unfounded rumor was that Belmont was actually an illegitimate Rothschild son. No one knew where he lived (some said he slept in his office). For the next fifty years New York Society would dance to whatever tune August Belmont chose to play.

Bessemer, Henry
1813-1898

"The Crazy Frenchman," Henry Bessemer experimented with steel and came home to Pittsburgh claiming, "The day of iron has passed-steel is king!"

The dazzling brilliance of the Bessemer converter transformed Andrew Carnegie into a new man. It wasn't long before 20,000 tons of steel rails rolled off the line each year.

Bezos, Jeff
1964-

Jeff Bezos was born in Texas. He went to Princeton and majored in electrical engineering and computer sciences, graduating Summa cum Laude. He moved to New York where he became the youngest vice president at Banker's Trust. At D.E. Shaw, an investment management firm, he met his future wife. It was also at Shaw that he got the idea for Amazon.

He was just thirty when he decided to quit his job and try to build an online bookstore. His wife Mackenzie told him to go for it.

It took Amazon more than six years to report its first quarterly profit at the end of 2001. Amazon is now the world's largest E- Commerce Company with revenues of more than $34.2 billion in 2010 and more than a billion in net profit.

Biddle, Nicholas
1786-1844

In 1823, Nicholas Biddle became President of The Second Bank of the United States. He was brilliant, debonair, and versatile. Biddle was descended from a distinguished Philadelphia family. He was a lawyer, a writer, and editor of the journal of The Lewis and Clark Expedition. He was also a state senator and a diplomat.

Biddle used the bank's reserves to help tide the country over the financial strain in 1825 and 1828. President Jackson never liked the National Bank. He believed that the bank's powers were too great. In 1841, The Second Bank of the United States closed its books.

Birdseye, Clarence
1886-1956

Clarence Birdseye's curiosity revolutionized the marketing of food in America. He wondered how Eskimos kept their food fresh. That led to a multi-billion dollar industry.

Birdseye was educated at Amherst. He worked as a fur trader in Labrador, and saw how Eskimos stored their meats and vegetables. He had an idea that fast freezing would seal in the freshness and taste of the food.

In 1929, Birdseye sold his patents, plants, and processes to the Postum Company for $22 million, which changed its name to General Foods. By 1934 Birdseye had 80 percent of the quick-frozen food business in America. By 1955, Americans were consuming more than $2 billion in frozen foods a year.

Blair, John Insley
1802-1899

John Blair was born in New Jersey. He was one of eleven children. He was so poor that he was determined to be rich. He built the largest railroad network of any individual. He controlled more than 2 million acres, becoming one of the richest men in America.

Blair started working in a country store when he was eleven. At 18 he had his own store. When he was 27 he owned five general stores and four flour mills. Blair then entered the coal and iron business. In 1846 he organized the Delaware, Lackawana & Western Railroad. Blair received the charter to build the Union Pacific Railroad, one of the last legs of the transcontinental railroad line.

Blair began building a network of railroads through about seven states and he was called "railroad king of the west." He owned more miles of railroad than any other individual in the world. At one time he was president of sixteen different railroads. He also put together sites for more than eighty towns along his routes.

Blair Hall in Princeton bears John Blair's name. He was on the board of trustees at Princeton. Blair lived 97 years. His energy was boundless and he traveled 40,000 miles a year surveying his railroad empire. He gave a great deal to charity and constructed more than 100 churches in the towns he built. His estate at the time of death was estimated at between $60 million and $80 million.

Blank, Arthur   **See Marcus, Bernie**

Bloomberg, Michael
1942-

Michael Bloomberg was born in Medford, Massachusetts. He put himself through Johns Hopkins and Harvard and became a partner at Salomon Brothers. Bloomberg started his own company which revolutionized the distribution of financial information and made him a billionaire. In 2002, Bloomberg became Mayor of New York City. He was elected to a second term and a controversial third term in 2009.

When Salomon Brothers was bought in 1981, Bloomberg started his own company. It was built around a financial information computer that revolutionized the way securities data was stored. The company was successful and soon branched out into the media business with more than 100 offices worldwide.

Bloomingdale, Lyman G.
1841-1905

Lyman Bloomingdale was an American businessman who, with his brother Joseph, founded Bloomingdales Department Store in New York City.
Lyman was the son of Benjamin Bloomingdale. He and his brother trained in retailing ladies clothing at their father's store. In 1886, they relocated operations to the present-day location at 59th Street and Third Avenue.
Joseph retired in 1896, and Lyman remained involved until his death in 1905.

Bluhdorn, Charles
1926-1983

The leader of a fast-growing conglomerate of the 1960s was Charles Bluhdorn, who started with an auto bumper manufacturer, Gulf & Western Industries. He had $8 million in sales and a net loss. By 1967 he had acquired more than eighty other companies, including Paramount Pictures, South Puerto Rico Sugar, and New Jersey Zinc, and earned $70 million on sales of $1.3 billion.
Bluhdorn was born in Vienna, son of a Czech-born importer. He came to the United States at sixteen, a refugee from Nazi anti-Semitism in 1942. He made his first million in his mid-twenties. Some of the other names in Gulf & Western's conglomerate were Desilu Productions, E.W. Bliss, and Consolidated Cigar.

Bluhdorn was flamboyant, fast-talking, with a Viennese accent. He hated vacations. He was considered to be among the wildest of the conglomerators, and the least restrained users of debt and convertible securities.

Boeing, William E.
1881-1956

The Boeing Company is an American multinational aerospace and defense corporation. It was founded in 1916 by William E. Boeing in Seattle, Washington. The company merged with McDonnell Douglas in 1997. Boeing is among the largest global aircraft manufacturers, and the third largest aerospace and defense contractor in the world.

The Boeing Airplane Company was named in 1917. After the United States entered World War I the U. S. needed seaplanes. After the war Boeing built commercial aircraft and built a successful airmail operation that evolved into United Airlines.

Boeing bought a shipyard in Seattle which later became his first airplane factory. Boeing and G.C. Westervelt built the B & W Seaplane and received an order from the Navy for fifty seaplanes. When the war ended military planes flooded the market and many companies went out of business. Boeing survived by building furniture, dressers, counters, and flat-bottom boats called sea sleds.

In 1934, The United States Government accused Boeing of monopolistic practices. William Boeing divested himself of ownership and his holding company United Aircraft and Transport Corporation broke into three separate entities:

- United Aircraft Corporation
- Boeing Airplane Company, which is now The Boeing Company
- United Airlines for flight operations

Boeing retired from the aircraft industry. He spent the remainder of his years in property development and thoroughbred horse breeding. William Boeing died in 1956, three days before his 75th birthday. He had a heart attack on his yacht. His ashes were scattered off the coast of British Columbia, where he spent much of his time sailing.

.

Borden, Gail
1801-1873

As a newspaperman, Gail Borden wrote the headline, "Remember the Alamo." On a trip from England he witnessed the death of immigrant babies who were drinking contaminated milk from diseased cows.

On his return to New York, Borden began to search for a method of removing the water from milk. He moved his family to New Lebanon, a Shaker community. They used a vacuum process to preserve fruit.

After two years, Borden had a new product which he called condensed milk. It was pure, fresh milk from which the water had been removed, and sugar was added. With difficulty, Gail Borden received a patent for his process in 1856. Although Borden has several occupations-a surveyor, a teacher, and a newspaperman, he was an inventor at heart. He was obsessed with the way to preserve food.

Jeremiah Milbank, a New York banker, invested $100,000 in the condensed milk business. When he died some years later, his investment was worth $8 million. Gail Borden died in 1873. His first factory employed three people and had sales of $48,000 the first year. By 1972, Borden, Inc. had worldwide sales of $22 billion. It had 47,000 employees, 7,500 products and 300 manufacturing locations. Borden's epitaph reads: "I tried and failed. I tried again and again, and succeeded."

Brady, "Diamond Jim" Buchanan
1856-1917

Jim Buchanan Brady was born in New York City. In 1899 he became an agent for The Pressed Steel Company. He loved jewels, especially diamonds. He collected precious stones which would be worth $50 million in 2005 dollars.

He loved food and could eat enough for 10 people. He was a long time friend of actress and singer Lillian Russell.

Brady accumulated about $12 million. He died in his sleep of a stroke in 1917.

Brandeis, Louis Dembitz
1856-1941

Louis Brandeis, the son of Jewish immigrants graduated first in his class from the Harvard Law School in 1877. Brandeis led investigations into monopoly-dominated industries including the railroad industry. J.P. Morgan had developed into an enemy of Brandeis, who championed public causes.

In 1916, Woodrow Wilson acknowledged Brandeis's contribution to social causes by naming him to the Supreme Court, the first Jew ever so named. The Pujo revelations and Brandeis's popular crusade against concentrated economic power helped to contribute to the Clayton Act of 1916. That legislation prohibited interlocking directorships. Thomas Lamont, a Morgan partner, stated before the senate committee investigating the stock exchange and investment banking in 1933 that Brandeis, in his book "Other People's Money" was behind the specific provision in the act.

Branson, Sir Richard
1950-

The flamboyant Sir Richard Branson quit school when he was fifteen and founded a magazine. It was the beginning of a successful career that includes Virgin Records, Virgin Airline, and Virgin Galactic. In July 2011, Branson announced that the space travel company had already taken 440 deposits from future space travelers, totaling $58 million dollars.

Branson doesn't buy companies, he starts them from scratch. When you are a small company you can move quicker. He believes in promoting from within. Bringing in executives from outside the company can be demoralizing. You make many mistakes, but hard work and will-power helps you keep paying the bills. "By daring to be disrespectful, we went from a $5 million overdraft facility to having a $40 million overdraft facility with a different bank. When one bank was willing to ruin us based on the assets we had, another bank was willing to give us more credit."

"There's a very thin dividing line between survival and failure. You've just got to fight and fight and fight and fight to survive."

Bronfman, Samuel
1889-1971

Born in Bessarabia, part of empirical Russia, now called Moldova, Samuel Bronfman was one of eight children of Mindel and Yechiel Bronfman. He and his family were refugees of Russia's anti-Semitic pogroms, who migrated to Saskatchewan, Canada. They soon moved to Manitoba.

The Bronfmans were a wealthy family who were tobacco farmers, but Canada was not compatible with its cold climate. Yechiel worked for the Canadian Northern Pacific Railway, and then in a sawmill. Eventually, Yechiel and his sons became involved in the hotel business.

Samuel noted that much of the profit was in the alcoholic beverages, so he set up shop as a liquor distributor. He founded Distiller's Corporation in Montreal in 1924, specializing in whiskey, and Samuel took advantage of prohibition in the United States, bootlegging to Boston, New York, and Chicago while operating in Canada.

The Bronfman Empire included Calvert, Dewars, and Seven Crown. His company was renamed Seagram Co. Ltd. Because of changes in the Lyndon Johnson administration it became advantageous for Bronfman to purchase an oil company. He did that by buying Texas Pacific Coal and Oil Company for $50 million in 1980. The Bronfman heirs sold Texas Pacific Oil to the Sun Oil Co. for $2.3 billion.

The Seagram assets have since been acquired by General Electric, Pepsico, Diageo, and Pernod Ricard.

Brown, Moses Henry
1738-1836

Moses Brown was the most eccentric of the premier families of Rhode Island business. He learned the art of bookkeeping from his uncle. He was one of four brothers.

Brown converted from a Baptist to a Quaker. He freed his slaves and became an abolitionist. In 1770 he brought Rhode Island College to Providence and it became Brown University in 1791. He was instrumental in founding the Providence Bank, the fifth commercial bank in the United State

Buffett, Warren Edward
1930

Warren Buffett is called, "The Sage of Omaha." He lives modestly in Omaha, Nebraska in a home he bought for $32,000. His staff is small, and he drives a vintage Lincoln.

Warren Buffett was born in Omaha in 1930. His father was a stockbroker. He started reading stock market books when he was eight. He began at eleven years of age as a stock boy, erasing and changing stock prices at Harris, Upham, where his dad worked.

IN 1965, Buffett acquired Berkshire Hathaway, a holding company for his investments. His investment strategy is to buy companies that an "idiot" can run. Coca Cola, American Express, and Gillette.

" I want to own good businesses, run by good managers."

Buffett presides over the annual shareholders' meetings. When asked how much of his great wealth he plans to pass on to his children?"

"Leave your children enough money so they can do something, but not do nothing."

Buffett's assets keep growing.

Busch, Adolphus
1839-1913

Adolphus Busch is a founder of the United States brewing industry. He established one of the leading beer companies. He built a family fortune and a corporate dynasty that continues to this day.

Busch was born in Mainz-on-the-Rhine, Germany, the youngest of twenty-one children. In 1857, at 18, Busch made the decision to come to America. He landed in St. Louis. When his father died he used a small inheritance to set up his own store selling brewer's supplies.

One of his customers was Eberhard Anheuser. In 1861, Adolphus and his brother Ulrich married Anheuser's two daughters. When his father-in-law died in 1879, the forty-year-old Adolphus became the president of the company.

Busch was a brilliant marketer. He created Budweiser Beer to add to the more expensive Michelob Brand. He also invested in real estate and banking. Everything he touched turned to gold. Before the days of income tax he was earning $2 million a year. When he died at the age of seventy-five, his $50 million estate was the largest ever probated in Missouri.

Carlson, Chester Floyd
1906-1968

Chester Carlson as a boy in California had to provide for his ailing parents. He worked his way through Cal Tech, worked for Bell Labs, and lost his job in the depression in 1933. He worked for a law firm, and then specialized in patent work.

Carlson decided there must be a better way to make copies of legal documents. He researched photo-electric, and dry means of copying. He patented a product in 1937, but could not get financial backing to develop it. Battelle Memorial Institute and Russell Dayton helped with a research project and a number of improvements.

After the war, a small Rochester, New York firm, The Haloid Company, was looking for new products. By 1947, Haloid had agreed to underwrite research in exchange for a license to manufacture the undeveloped machine. It was 1950, and the machine was developed for the process known as xerography. In 1955 Haloid sales rose to $21 million. The company name was changed to Haloid Xerox, and in 1961 to the Xerox Corporation. Revenues rose to $100 million in 1962, and rose to far above $1 billion by the end of the decade.

Carnegie, Andrew
1835-1919

Andrew Carnegie was an ambitious Scot who rose from obscurity to become a giant in the steel industry. He had made millions before the 1873 Panic. He gained control of the Iron City Forge Company. Carnegie founded the forerunner of Carnegie Steel to use the Bessemer Steel Process and shrewdly called the new plant the Edgar Thomson Works after the President of the Pennsylvania Railroad. The reason for that was no secret. One of Carnegie's best customers was that huge railroad with its unlimited need for steel rails and other products.

The sale of Carnegie Steel to J.P. Morgan for $492 million was a boon to the country's readers because Carnegie willed $350 million to build thousands of libraries.

As a boy of fourteen Carnegie was a bobbin boy in a cloth mill. He worked 12 hours a day in a dank cellar. However, he was excited about the optimism of his new country. He wrote his Scotch friends, "Everything was in motion-railroads-telegraph-canals. Pauperism is unknown."

The success of Andrew Carnegie is legend. His legacy will never die. His money has benefitted millions of Americans. Carnegie-Mellon University and thousands of libraries give meaning to Carnegie's epitaph: "He who dies rich dies disgraced."

Carrier, Willis Haviland
1876-1950

Dr. Willis Carrier is considered the father of air conditioning. He launched the cooling industry in 1922. His new cooling machine used a centrifugal compressor with a safe refrigerant. It was not long before Dr. Carrier's machine had created a huge new market for comfort air conditioning.

By 1930, 293 centrifugal refrigeration machines had been sold to provide cooling for skyscrapers, stores, the House and Senate Chambers in Washington, the Battleship U.S.S. Wyoming, and Madison Square Garden.

The air conditioning industry has come as long way since Dr. Carrier introduced his revolutionary water chiller in 1922. It is a multi-billion dollar industry that provides the comfort that we expect in restaurants, movie theaters, and in our homes.

Clark, William Andrews
1839-1925

William Andrews Clark made his fortune in Montana copper mines. He became a United States senator and a founder of the state of Montana and one of its most prominent citizens. Clark was born in Pennsylvania and his family moved to Iowa when he was seventeen. He soon became a teacher, but he was drawn to the gold and silver mines of Colorado when he was twenty-three.

Clark opened a general store in the Montana territory. He used his growing fortune to buy into several abandoned gold mines. He took a year off to study mining, geology, and mineralogy. He learned that gold miners were throwing away valuable copper and silver tailings. Clark used his earnings to move into banking, real estate, timber, water power, and cattle ranching. He became a millionaire at the age of 34.

His bitter rival was Marcus Daly who discovered the highly profitable Anaconda Mine. Clark backed an unknown, Thomas H. Carter to defeat Daly for the senate seat. However, in 1895 Clark won the senate seat with what was described as $430,000 in bribes to the Montana legislature. Clark was forced to resign in the scandal that ensued. He was later appointed by Montana's acting Governor to fill an unexpired term and then won reelection in 1901.

Clark built a $7 million house on 5th Avenue after his first wife died. He took in a "ward" of seventeen. He moved her to Paris where she bore him two children. Five years later he married her. His $150 million fortune was left to his eight children.

Clinton, DeWitt
1769-1828

New York Governor DeWitt Clinton was an early advocate of a canal from the Hudson River to Lake Erie. "Clinton's Ditch" was completed in 1825 at a cost of $8.4 million.

The Erie Canal accelerated the movement of goods. Freight rates dropped and the time of shipment was cut sharply. Today, most of the canals are only muddy memories of their past glory. But in their prime, they did more to cut freight costs and knit the country's regions together than any other aid to transport.

Colgate, William
1783-1857

In 1803, William Colgate became an apprentice in a soap factory. He established his own business. Three years later, his sons and nephews joined the business, and the completion of The Erie Canal opened the West to his thriving enterprise.

By 1906, the firm was making 160 different kinds of soaps and toiletries. In 1928 Colgate merged with the Palmolive-Peet Company. The Baptist Education Society of New York started a school in 1820, near Hamilton, New York. Colgate gave so much money to the school that by 1890 half the endowment stemmed from Colgate's fortune. The college changed the name to Colgate.

Colt, Samuel
1814-1862

Born in Hartford, Connecticut in 1814, Colt got his first patent in England in 1835. He founded The Patent Arms Manufacturing Co. in Paterson, New Jersey. The company soon fell into bankruptcy. The Mexican War saved Colt. The Texas Rangers ordered 1,000 "arms" at $25, and the second thousand at $17.50.

Colt adapted mass-production and Henry Leland used the technique to manufacture automobiles (the Cadillac) in Michigan. Colt soon became a millionaire and built the greatest mid-nineteenth century arms plant in the world. He was a pioneer in employee relations. He lowered the workday from fourteen hours to ten. He built the first social center for employees and provided his men with hot water, soap, and towels.

Cooke, Jay
1821-1905

Jay Cooke was the banker who sold bonds to finance the Union Army during the Civil War. He went to the wall in the Panic of 1873, and thirty-seven banks and brokerage houses went with him. Daniel Drew was caught with a load of stocks and it marked his demise in Wall Street. He was $1 million dollars in debt. The attempt to complete the Northern Pacific Railroad was the cause of Jay Cooke's fall.

Jay Cooke was the great government bond salesman of the Civil War. He was affable, outgoing, and optimistic. Cooke set up a national organization of banks, insurance companies, and individuals, backing them with paper advertising, posters, handbills, and publicity. In this way he managed the successful sale of more than $1 billion worth of bonds.

Cooper, Peter
1791-1883

Peter Cooper was an industrialist whose youthful experience left him with a craving for education. He worked with his father from the age of eight. He made hats, tried brick-making, and brewing, and left his father and went to New York City.

Cooper apprenticed as a coach-maker and designed a cloth-shearing machine. He sold the rights to Matthew Vassar, who eventually endowed a college for women. He used the proceeds to buy real estate and a glue factory. In 1828, Cooper bought 3,000 acres in the City of Baltimore for $105,000. Cooper built the "Tom Thumb," a steam engine which saved the Baltimore and Ohio Railroad from bankruptcy.

In 1854, Cooper was president of a company that laid the cable across the Atlantic Ocean to Great Britain. In 1856, his net worth was more than a million dollars, but he felt handicapped by his lack of a formal education.

He founded and built the Cooper Union in 1859 and presented it to the people of New York City. To this day, it offers free education in the Arts and Sciences.

Cornell, Ezra.
1807-1874

Ezra Cornell was born in the Bronx. His family moved to upstate New York, and he settled in Ithaca, where he later founded Cornell University.

Cornell was a carpenter and he served as a state senator from 1864 to 1867. He was a Quaker and he was disowned by the Society of Friends for marrying outside the faith.

Cornell stated, "I have always considered that choosing a companion for life was a very important affair, and that my happiness or misery in this life depended on the choice."

Cornell made his fortune in the telegraph business as an associate of Samuel Morse. He constructed telegraph poles between Washington D.C. and Baltimore. It was the first ever telegraph line of substance in the United States. He built many other lines including one from Buffalo to Milwaukee.

Ezra Cornell founded Western Union and received 2 million shares of stock. Eventually, he retired and dedicated himself to philanthropy. He founded Cornell University and his sarcophagus is in the Sage Chapel.

Crocker, Charles
1822-1888

Charles Crocker, the last of the big four, came to California from Indiana with his younger brother during the 1849 Gold Rush. He worked in Placer Mines and then he opened a store in Sacramento. He was elected to the state legislature.

The four Sacramento merchants backed a project to build a railroad into the silver-mining country. The partners had no experience with railroads, but they invested $35,000 into the Central Pacific Railroad. The Pacific Railway Act in 1862 granted the Central Pacific the right to meet the Union Pacific Railroad. The Central Pacific was moving east from Sacramento and the Union Pacific was moving west from Omaha.

The big four worked well together. Huntington handled Washington, Stanford was elected Governor of California in 1861. Crocker oversaw construction, and Hopkins managed the books. It took 10,000 Chinese workers who got $1 a day to meet the tracks of the Union Pacific at Promontory, Utah, where the Golden Spike was hammered home.

Charles Crocker, who built a fortune of $20 to $40 million, was seriously injured in a carriage accident in 1886. He never fully recovered and died two years later.

Crown, Henry
1896-1990

Henry Crown was an American industrialist and philanthropist. He founded the Material Service Corporation, which merged with General Dynamics in 1959. When he died in 1990 he was a billionaire. Henry Crown & Company is an investment firm that has interests in a variety of business assets.

Crown (birth name was Henry Krinsky) was born in 1896. He was the third of seven children of a sweatshop worker, Arie Krinsky, and his wife Ida. His name was changed when Henry was a boy.

In 1919, with borrowed capital of $10,000, Crown and his brother Irving established The Material Service Corporation. MSC sold gravel, sand, lime, and coal to builders in the Chicago area. In 1959 Crown merged his company with General Dynamics. According to his own claim, Henry Crown had given away "nine figures" in his philanthropic pursuits by the time he was 79. His beneficiaries included The University of Chicago, Brandeis, Stanford, Northwestern, and the St. Lawrence University Investment Fund.

Cullman, Frederick Joseph III
1912-2004

Frederick Joseph Cullman III was the CEO of Phillip Morris from 1957-1970. His brother was Edgar Cullman Sr., who was Chairman of the Culbro Corporation, the parent company of General Cigar. General Cigar manufactured Macanudo, Partagas, Temple Hall, Ramon Allons, and the Garcia Vega brand. It also owned the U.S. rights to Bolivar, Cifuentes, and Cohibas Cigars.

Edgar Cullman Jr. now heads the Culbro Corporation. He manages the many real estate interests of the company and the General Cigar Corporation has been sold.

Curtis, Cyrus H. K.
1850-1933

Cyrus Curtis founded the Ladies Home Journal and bought The Saturday Evening Post for $1,000 in 1897. Curtis was born in Portland, Maine in 1850. His family lost everything in the Great Portland Fire in 1866. Cyrus was forced to leave high school. When he was nineteen he worked in a dry-goods store in Boston. He then sold advertising for newspapers. He established his own paper. This led to The Ladies Home Journal. Within a year the circulation rose to 100,000.

After buying the Saturday Evening Post in 1897, The Post at 5 cents a copy became the largest selling weekly magazine in the world, with a circulation of more than 3 million. When Curtis died, the circulation of the Ladies Home Journal reached 2.5 million.

Curtis was almost eighty-three when he died, and he had a fortune estimated at $174 million from his publishing enterprises.

Curtiss, Glenn
1878-1930

Glenn Curtiss was an American aviation pioneer and a founder of the U.S. aircraft industry. He began as a bicycle racer and a builder of motorcycles. In 1906 he manufactured engines for airships.

Curtiss made the first witnessed flight in North America. He also won a race at the world's first international air show in France, and made the first long-distance flight in the United States. Curtiss designed and built aircraft and formed the Curtiss Airplane and Motor Company, now part of the Curtiss-Wright Corporation. His company built aircraft for the U.S. Army and Navy during World War I. Curtiss aircraft were predominant during World War II.

Curtiss was born in Hammondsport, New York. He only went to school until the eighth grade. He worked for the company which became Eastman Kodak. He was married and had two children. In 1903 he set a record of 136.36 miles per hour on a 40 horsepower V8 motorcycle of his own design and construction. He was the fastest man in the world until 1930. His success strengthened his reputation as a leader of high performance motorcycles and engines.

Curtiss designed the famous "June-bug" and became its test pilot. In 1908 he flew 5,080 feet and won a $2,500 prize. In 1910, Curtiss demonstrated a flight from the deck of a Naval Cruiser. It was the precursor of modern day carrier operations. Curtiss was the first Naval aviator. During World War I The Curtiss Company sold thousands of aircraft to the militaries of the United States, Canada, and Great Britain. The company grew to employ 18,000 workers. After the war contracts were canceled. Glenn Curtiss cashed out his stock in the company for $32 million and retired to Florida.

The Wright Company merged with Curtiss to form the Curtiss-Wright Company just before Curtiss's death. Curtiss and his family moved to Florida in the 1920s. He founded 18 corporations. Curtiss suffered an attack of appendicitis in court. He died in 1930 in Buffalo, New York of complications from an appendectomy.

Danforth, William H.
1870-1955

William H. Danforth founded Nestle Purina in St.Louis, Missouri in 1894. Ralston's checkerboard logo evolved from a personal development concept Danforth put forth in his book, "I Dare You," in which he used a checkerboard to explain it.

Danforth proposed that four key components in life need to be in balance. "Physical" was on the left, "Mental" on top, "Social" on the right, and "Religious" was on the bottom. To be healthy, you needed the four squares to stay in balance. The concept became intertwined with the company in 1921, when it began selling feed that was pressed in cubes called "Checkers."

Danforth's son was Donald, a former chief executive of the company. His grandsons include former U.S. Senator John Danforth.

Davis, Arthur Vining
1867-1962

Arthur Vining Davis built the Aluminum Corporation of America and made $400 million in the process. Davis was born in 1867, the son of a minister in a town near Boston. He graduated from Amherst. In 1888, his father got him a job in Pittsburgh. The company was called the Pittsburgh Reduction Company. Davis earned $60 a month. The founder, Charles Marvin Hall invented a new process for manufacturing aluminum cheaply. Aluminum was a lighter alternative to iron, steel, and other metals. The first batch of commercial aluminum was produced in 1888. The problem was that no one wanted to buy it.

Davis had two powerful backers—Andrew and Richard Mellon. When Hall died in 1914 Davis assumed control of the company. When he retired in 1957, Davis was the third richest individual in the world. He then went to Florida and began building resorts. He owned one-eighth of Dade County.

Davis, who started as a penniless preacher's son worked his way up to a fortune of $400 million. However, it might have been much more, because as Davis said, "Who has time to add it up?"

Deere, John
1801-1886

John Deere founded the agricultural machinery company that bears his name. He traveled westward from Vermont where he was a blacksmith. Deere fashioned his first plow from a circular saw blade of Sheffield Steel.

American made steel accelerated his business and he moved to Moline on the Mississippi where he could transport his plows by water.

Today, more than a billion dollars' worth of Deere agricultural machinery is sold each year. It is one of the largest industrial firms in America.

Depew, Chauncey M.
1834-1928

Chauncey Depew was an attorney for Commodore Cornelius Vanderbilt's railroad interests. He was President of the New York Central Railroad System, and was a United States Senator from New York from 1894 to 1911.

Depew was born in 1834 and attended Peekskill Military Academy for 12 years. He went to Yale and was a member of Skull and Bones. He practiced law in Peekskill, entered the brokerage business, and he declined an appointment as minister to Japan in 1865 to pursue his railroad interests.

Depew became general counsel and director of the whole "Vanderbilt System." In 1898 he served as Chairman of the Board of Directors of the New York Central Railroad Company. He also served on the boards of many other companies.

Chauncey Depew was a great orator. He was married twice and had a son from his first marriage, Chauncey Mitchell Depew Jr. The village of Depew, New York and Depew, Oklahoma are named in his honor. He died at the age of 94 in 1928. His "My Autobiography" in 1922 and his speeches on the threshold of 92 in 1925 summed up a full life of service and contributions to the development of this country.

Disney, Walter Elias
1901-1966

Walt Disney was a film producer, director, screenwriter, etc. He was an international icon. He founded Walt Disney Productions. The Walt Disney Company had annual revenues in 2010 of $36 billion.

Walt Disney created Mickey Mouse, Donald Duck, and many other well-known fictional characters. He died of lung cancer in 1966. One year later the Walt Disney World Resort "Disneyland" was built in Florida.

Dorrance John T.
1873-1930

Dr. John T. Dorrance made Campbell Soups a fixture of American life. Dorrance was born in Pennsylvania. He graduated from MIT in 1895, and earned a Ph.D. in Chemistry from the University of Goettingen, Germany in just two years.

Dorrance was a brilliant chemist. He joined his uncle at the Campbell Preserve Company in Camden, New Jersey. Although they had 200 products, they had no soup. He worked for his uncle at a salary of $7.50 a week.

In 1899, the 26 year-old Dorrance developed a process for removing water from soup. The first varieties were tomato, consommé, vegetable, chicken, and oxtail. Soup was popular in Europe, but Americans had to adapt to the custom. At 10 cents a can, Campbell's became an instant success by 1904. By 1914, Dorrance's company was selling sixteen million cans of soup.

Dorrance was named president of the company in 1914 and held that position until his death in 1930. When his uncle retired, he sold Dorrance his share of the business for $755,720. Dorrance became the sole owner less than 20 years after joining the company.

The business continued to grow. In 1927 the company had $50 million in sales. It was selling ten million cans of soup per day. John Dorrance died at the age of 56 in 1930. His fortune was $115 million, which made him the third richest man in America. He had four daughters and a son.

John T. Dorrance Jr. took charge of the company and continued to expand the business. He added C.A. Swanson in 1955, Pepperidge Farm in 1961, and Vlasic Foods.

Dow, Charles
1851-1902

Charles Dow is a Wall Street legend. He created the financial bible, The Wall Street Journal, and the first market barometer, the Dow-Jones Averages. He died at the age of 51.

Dow began compiling his stock market averages in 1884, before The Wall Street Journal existed. The Dow Theory, as we know it today, was refined and developed from Dow's editorials twenty years after his death by other market technicians like William P. Hamilton and Robert Rhea.

Dow was born in Connecticut in 1851. His father died when he was six. He found his niche in financial writing while working for a newspaper in Providence, Rhode Island. He founded Dow-Jones & Co. in 1882 with Eddie Jones. They had a one-room office at 15 Wall Street.

There were about 35 major stocks and several hundred companies at the time, and Charles Dow created an authoritative standard by which we can measure the market. We still use that standard today. That function alone insures Dow a place in The Wall Street Hall of Fame.

Drew, Daniel
1797-1879

Preacher Daniel Drew was an engineer of panics. He was a famous bear. The king of the bears died penniless and broken-hearted in the arms of one of his few remaining friends. But, in his prime, as Treasurer of the Erie, he amassed the most cash of anyone in his time--$13 million dollars.

Drew was unbeatable until he met Jay Gould and Jim Fisk. He said of Gould, "His touch is death." In his book, "Fifty Years in Wall Street," Henry Clews recalls a dinner when Drew was at his peak. All the speakers glorified him. Five years later Drew was finished and broke. His bankruptcy schedule included a watch and chain valued at $150, a Sealskin coat $150, wearing apparel $100, and a bible and hymn books, etc. $130.

Drew on the 18th of September 1869, Drew on the 18th of September 1879. What a contrast! Then, rich, powerful, with troops of friends and retainers! Now, penniless, broken-hearted, and away from home, he dies in the arms of one of his few remaining friends.

Dreyfus, Jack (John J.)
1913-2009

Jack Dreyfus was an American financial expert and the founder of the Dreyfus Fund. He was born in Alabama and graduated from Lehigh University in Pennsylvania. He invented the direct marketing of mutual funds to the public. His early television commercials featuring a lion emerging from the Wall Street subway station were successful. Barron's end of century issue considered Jack Dreyfus the second most significant money manager of the last century.

Dreyfus married Joan Personette in 1939. They were divorced and had one child—John (Johnny). His paternal grandfather was a first cousin of Alfred Dreyfus, the French officer who was the subject of the anti-Semitic Dreyfus Affair in the 19th century.

In the early 1960s Dreyfus established Hobeau Farm in Ocala, Florida, where he bred, trained, and raced thoroughbred racehorses. He sold the property in 2005 for $12,750,000. His horses beat the famous horse Seabiscuit in the Whitney Stakes and the Woodward Stakes in 1973.

John (Jack) Dreyfus died in 2009 at the age of 95.

Duke, James B.
1856-1925

James Buchanan Duke was a poor Carolina farm boy. Bright leaf tobacco was grown on his farm. In 1881 he designed a cigarette-making machine that could turn out 200 cigarettes a minute. By 1889 "Buck" was selling 800 million cigarettes annually. He captured 38 percent of the market.

In 1890, five principal tobacco manufacturers joined to form the American Tobacco Company. Duke also joined with the British to found the British-American Tobacco Company. Duke got two-thirds of the stock. At that point, Duke's holdings included 150 factories capitalized at $502 million.

American Tobacco was ordered dissolved by the Supreme Court in 1911. By that time Duke had established a $100 million trust fund that helped create Trinity College (later named Duke University).

DuPont, Eleuthere, Irenee
1771-1834

Irenee DuPont made his name synonymous with gunpowder. He came to America in 1800 as an apprentice to the great chemist, Lavoisier. He established a gunpowder factory in Wilmington, Delaware. Thomas Jefferson gave him his first order in 1801.

For many years the business was strapped. However, when DuPont died in 1834, he was worth $317,124, and his mills were producing 1,000,000 pounds of explosives a year. In 1818, an explosion killed forty of his men. DuPont provided for all the victims' families.

In 1951 DuPont's average investment was worth over $1,500,000,000---5,000 times as much as in 1834. DuPont is one of the outstanding blue chip companies in America.

Durant, William Crapo
1861-1947

William Durant made his first million selling carriages. He knew nothing about automobiles. In 1908, Durant incorporated General Motors, with a capitalization of $12 million. When David Buick ran out of money, Durant took over. His General Motors bought Cadillac, Oakland, Weston, and Oldsmobile. He tried to add Ford and Maxwell to the combination but a J.P. Morgan partner turned him down when he tried to add more capital.

Within two years General Motors was on the verge of bankruptcy. Bankers took control and replaced Durant with Charles Nash, who made Walter Chrysler head of the Buick division. Durant was not through. He got financing from Louis Chevrolet, and Durant increased his stock holdings in General Motors until he had a commanding position there.

In 1915, Durant became acquainted with DuPont through a son-in-law, who was made President of Chevrolet. In 1917 DuPont bought $25 million of General Motors stock, and continued to increase their investment. They shared control of the company and eventually took over completely. This happened on the advice of financial wizard John Jakob Raskob. It became the keystone of the DuPont fortune.

Alfred P. Sloan was put in charge of GM by the DuPont's. He said, "Durant could create, but not administer." So the man who would have been the richest man in the world, was ruined financially, and was said to have owned a diner in New Jersey. It was hardly a just end for a prime mover of the 1920s and the founder of General Motors.

Durant was one of the greats. He would have been worth $500 million and would have retained control of General Motors had he not speculated. He owed $27 million, three banks and twenty-seven brokerage houses were involved. If nothing had been done, the banks and several brokers would have failed. The DuPonts and Morgans came in and took over his General Motors holdings. (They Told Barrons)

Eames, Francis L.
1844-1898

More than one hundred years after the Buttonwood
Tree Agreement of 1792, a thoroughly detailed account of
the New York Stock Exchange was constructed by Francis
Eames, its president in 1894. His admission that he
undertook the task of compiling the history with reluctance
underscores the reality that his descriptions consist of facts
that he could not possibly relate, the color and feeling of
those early days as well as could one of the original
members. Historians can be grateful to Eames, for his
endeavor has faithfully recorded the scenes and conditions
which are historically interesting, and will always stand as
a factual record of the humble beginnings of the New York
Stock Exchange.

Eastman, George
1854-1932

Photography, first confined to professionals, began to catch on in the United States after George Eastman read in an English Almanac about a means of cutting the size and weight of camera equipment. He patented a paper-backed film in 1884, and started a hand-held camera company after concocting a distinctive name for it, The Kodak. He sold the camera with enough film for 100 exposures, after which the camera and film were returned to the factory for developing, printing, and reloading. "You press the button—we do the rest," Eastman advertised.

In January 2002, the Eastman Kodak Company declared bankruptcy. The digital camera onslaught had taken its toll.

Eaton, Cyrus Stephen
1883-1979

Cyrus Eaton was born in Nova Scotia. His father had a small general store. Eaton became an American investment banker, businessman, and philanthropist, with a career that spanned seventy years.

For decades Eaton was one of the most powerful financiers in the American Midwest. He was a colorful and controversial figure. He was known for his longevity in business and his opposition to the dominance of Eastern financiers in the America of his day. For his occasionally ruthless financial manipulations, and his outspoken criticism of the United States cold war policy. He founded and helped organize the First Pugwash Conferences on World Peace in 1955.

Eaton, Joseph Oriel II
1829-1875

Joseph Eaton developed truck axles in Bloomfield, New Jersey. He sold seven axles in the first year. He was the son of an Ohio farmer. Eaton graduated from Williams College in 1895. He held a variety of jobs before he got around to making truck axles.

Eaton's company grew and he moved to Cleveland to be near truck manufacturers. The Eaton Manufacturing Company merged with Yale & Towne in 1966. Eaton has expanded into many fields. It is a tribute to his foresight that no car or truck made in the United States comes off the assembly line without some Eaton manufactured parts in it. Joe Eaton, a one-time $8-a-week clerk had a good idea, and another success story was born.

Edison, Thomas Alva
1847-1931

It would be difficult to figure how much money was made with the inventions of Thomas Edison. He invented the light bulb, the phonograph, the motion picture, and so many other items. When Congress awarded Edison a gold medal for his service to humanity, legislators figured that his inventions were worth almost $16 billion. Thomas Edison made quite a bit of money and he was well off. At his death he was worth $12 million.

Thomas Edison was born in Ohio in 1847. He turned out to be one of the most prolific inventors in America. He learned telegraph dispatching and was an operator for five years. He invented an automatic vote recorder, a unison stop device for stock tickers, a mimeograph machine, etc. However, the greatest feat Edison achieved was the invention of the incandescent lamp.

The Edison Electric Light Company morphed into the General Electric Company, and the world has Thomas Alva Edison to thank for the convenience of electric lights which light up our homes, our businesses, and our cities.

Ellison, Lawrence J.
1944-

Larry Ellison has always been compared to Bill Gates. They both dropped out of college and founded software companies. Ellison's fortune is less than one-third the size of Microsoft. Revenues of Oracle are one-half those of Bill Gates' company. Ellison was so impressed with the Japanese that he built a Japanese house. He is attracted to the Samurai, who were cultured warriors.

Born in 1944 in Chicago, his unwed mother gave Ellison to a great aunt in California, to raise him. She didn't see him for 45 years. Larry tracked her down. His Russian immigrant relatives gave him the name Ellison from Ellis Island, where they arrived in New York.

Handsome, eccentric, Ellison found Silicon Valley and worked as a programmer. He started on his own with a $1,200 investment and $400 from a partner in 1977. Ellison bet on the shift from main-frames to microcomputers. By 1990, Ellison had a $1 billion company. In 1994 it reached $2 billion.

Ellison has been married and divorced three times. He has a reputation as a ladies' man. He is not content to be the number two company in the world. "We want to be number one!" says Lawrence Ellison.

Evans, Oliver
1755-1819

Oliver Evans devised a machine-driven wonder in 1790. The Delaware-born mechanical genius eliminated human labor from the process of turning grain into flour.

His apparatus was able to receive the grain from the wagon or ship, to elevate and convey it, until it was placed over the mill stones to be ground. In short, it performed the whole operation of turning grain into flour ready for packing.

With his automatic flour mill, six men could turn 100,000 bushels of grain into flour in a year.

Fargo, William George
1818-1881

William G. Fargo was a co-founder of the American Express Company and Northwestern National Bank in Minneapolis, and served as Mayor of Buffalo, New York. The city of Fargo, North Dakota is named in his honor.

Both Henry Wells and William G. Fargo began their careers as express men in upstate New York before joining forces with other express operators in 1845 to extend their business to Chicago and St. Louis, the western edge of what was then the United States.

Business was plentiful for the company with the expansion of the railroads. Gold was discovered in California in 1848 and California achieved statehood in 1850. On March 18, 1852 Wells, Fargo & Co. was born.

Ferkauf, Eugene
1920-2012

Starting with a $4,000 investment in a retail store, Eugene Ferkauf brought discount pricing into department-type stores in the East. By following the great migration of the middle-class into the suburbs, seeking high traffic locations, and minimizing markups, Ferkauf built his Korvette store chain to a gross of $55 million in 1956, and then launched an expansion program and sold 1,000,000 shares of stock to the public.

Korvette's sales volume moved up to $100 million in 1961, and to $800 million in 1966, making E.J. Korvette one of the nation's leaders in the general merchandise field.

Field, Marshall
1834-1906

Marshall Field made most of his fortune in real estate. In 1839, a quarter-acre downtown cost $20. By 1894, the same piece of land was worth $1.25 million. Field who had purchased downtown land at bargain prices was soon sitting on a fortune.

The son of a Massachusetts farmer, Marshall Field came to Chicago at the age of twenty-one to work in a dry-goods house. He joined Lech Z. Leiter and Potter Palmer to found a dry-goods store. Field bought out his partners to found Marshall Field & Co. He lost two stores in the Chicago Fire of 1871 and again in 1877. He rebuilt the stores and they kept growing. Shortly after his death Field's company did $68 million a year. Marshall Field & Co. opened the largest store in the world in downtown Chicago, with 450 departments on 78 acres with 13 floors.

Marshall Field's personal life was less fortunate than his business career. His family chose to live abroad and his son shot himself one year before his father's death. Field's $145 million fortune was bequeathed to his two grandsons, Marshall Field III and Henry Field. Marshall Field III entered the newspaper business and amassed a fortune of $168 million.

Filene, William
1830-1901

William Filene was born in Posen, then in Prussia, in 1830 and he came to America when he was eighteen years old. He started working in Boston as a tailor. When he was 21 he opened a small dry-goods store. It had little success. By 1856, Filene was in Salem and he had married Clara Ballin, a German immigrant, who became the mother of his four sons and a daughter.

After the Panic of 1873, Filene opened four stores, two in Lynn, one in Salem, and another in Bath, Maine. When William Filene was sixty, he built the largest women's wear store in Boston and retired. He yielded the management of the business to his sons, Edward and Lincoln. The name of the company was changed to William Filene's Sons Company. William Filene died in 1901.

Fisk, James Jr. (Jubilee Jim)
1834-1872

After a partnership in a Boston jobbing house, Jim Fisk received a large bonus and he moved to New York. He lost all his money in Wall Street. A subsequent litigation was very profitable and "Fisk and Belden" set up shop as brokers. The Erie manipulators are legend, and Jim Fisk was allied with Jay Gould in 1869, trying to corner the gold market. Fisk had a great mind and originated genuinely sensational measures.

Fisk was sued by a former mistress. She claimed that he failed to continue to pay her sums of money they had agreed upon earlier, that later amounted to blackmail. One afternoon as Fisk was leaving the courtroom, he was shot several times by the woman's current lover. He died shortly thereafter.

Flint, Charles R. Jr.
1850-1934

Charles Flint was an active promoter of business combinations. In 1911, he consolidated Herman Hollerith's Tabulating Machines Company into a group of computing scale and time-recording companies. The Computing Tabulating-Recording Company needed capable management.

In 1914, Flint hired forty-year old Thomas J. Watson, who had been a crackerjack salesman and sales manager for the National Cash Register Co. Watson reshaped the firm. He started a research division with his friend Charles Kettering and improved Herman Hollerith's machine. IBM sales passed the $1 billion mark in 1951.

Ford, Henry Sr.
1863-1947

A young Detroit mechanic named Henry Ford was born on a Michigan farm in 1863. By day, he was a $45 a month mechanic. By evening, he was building a new auto. After failing twice, he finally brought out an automobile that would sell for as little as $490 in 1914, the Model T. By 1916, Ford was selling 4 million cars, one-sixth of all the auto sales in the United States.

Franklin, Benjamin
1706-1790

Benjamin Franklin is one of our founding fathers. He led an exemplary life and was one of the most prominent men of his time-a critical force in the establishment of the nation. He was a pioneer in science, education, and government. He invented bifocals and the Franklin stove.

Franklin was born in 1706, the son of a Boston soap and candle maker. He became a printer and his fortune was gained by buying houses in Philadelphia before the revolution. He also bought land in Boston, Nova Scotia, Georgia, and Ohio.

Franklin opened a print shop in 1728. He started the Pennsylvania Gazette and Poor Richard's Almanac. He built the first Fire Company, Free library, Insurance Company, University, and Hospital. He was Governor of Pennsylvania. No salary. Franklin became Ambassador to France and was there for six years.

History has been kind to Benjamin Franklin. He is often quoted with his "a penny saved is a penny earned." He lived a useful life and he died rich as well.

Frick, Henry Clay
1849-1919

Henry Frick was born in 1849 in western Pennsylvania. His grandfather was Abraham Overholt, the whiskey distiller of "Old Overholt." Frick was small, engaged in no active sports as a boy, and had almost no friends. His sole desire was to emulate his grandfather and become a millionaire.

Early in his career, Frick began to accumulate land in the Connellsville Region, which had great seams of bituminous coal, which is used in the "coking" process for smelting pig iron ore into steel by the Bessemer method. In 1871, the young Frick asked Judge Thomas Mellon for $10,000 at 10 percent to build fifty coke ovens. Mellon granted the loan, and Frick was on his way. During the Panic of 1873, Frick continued to buy coal lands, and he survived to become the owner of 80 percent of the coke business. At the age of thirty Frick was a millionaire.

Carnegie was Frick's best customer and it was only natural for the two to join forces. The union of Carnegie and Frick companies in 1883 created a "vertical" combination that was an economic juggernaut which dominated the American steel industry.

Fulton, Robert
1765-1815

No history of the steamboat era would be complete without the contribution of Robert Fulton. With Livingston, Fulton obtained a twenty-year steamboat monopoly of New York State waters. Afterward he got a franchise for the lower Mississippi.

Fulton wrote to President Jefferson, that within a few years his steamboats would be operating on the Hudson, the Mississippi, the Delaware, the Ohio, and the St. Lawrence.

Eventually, Cornelius Vanderbilt built his own steamboats in 1829, and by 1836 he had built a fortune of $500,000 at the age of forty-two. Before he turned to railroads he had become one of the largest steamboat builders in the country.

Fulton's first steam-powered boat," The Clermont" proved successful in 1807. It sparked great support for shipping, but new forms of transportation were developed in the United States that would challenge shipping within a few decades.

Gates, Bill
1955-

One of the greatest business stories of all time started in 1975 when Bill Gates and his friend Paul Allen saw a magazine which had a story about a computer called the Altair 8800.

They thought about the software that could be done for it. Not only did Paul Allen get a deal with the company, he was hired as vice president of software. Gates dropped out of Harvard and Microsoft was born.

Their big break came in 1980 when IBM made one of the biggest blunders in the history of business. IBM turned to Microsoft to develop the operating system for the soon to be launched personal computer. IBM thought the value would be in the hardware.

The PC era was here and Gates and Allen had one of the most valuable contracts ever drafted. Part of the deal restricted IBM's ability to compete with Microsoft in licensing the MS-DOS operating system to other computer makers.

It was a brilliant stroke that outmaneuvered IBM and laid the groundwork that created the company's massive success. IBM's mistake allowed Bill Gates to grow from a back-room start-up into the world's largest software company, which was worth at its peak, $400 billion.

With his great wealth, Bill Gates has created a foundation, and has devoted his life to funding the development of vaccines to save lives throughout the world. As of this writing, Bill Gates is the richest man in the world, with a total of $71 billion dollars in assets.

Gates, John (Bet-a-Million)
1855-1911

Farmers who moved into the wide-open prairie spaces encountered two major shortages—water and fencing materials. The answer was wells and barbed wire, which was patented by two Illinois farmers. Sales grew from 10,000 pounds in 1874 to more than 80 million pounds in 1880.

A leading salesman was John (Bet-a-Million) Gates. He started a whirlwind of sales that ended with Gates as head of American Steel and Wire Company.

Geneen, Harold Sydney
1910-1997

Harold Geneen was the builder of a massive conglomerate, International Telephone and Telegraph Corporation (IT&T). He developed a corporate empire and his salary (with bonus) was $812,494—the largest in the nation.

IT&T moved into the ranks of the top ten industrial companies by way of the merger route. Geneen expanded the company's communications interests, but he spread into other areas. He acquired Bell & Gosset, Avis, Sheraton Corp. and Levitt & Sons. He had to dispose of Avis and Levitt to retain Hartford Fire Insurance Company. In 1970, IT&T had sales of $6.4 billion, almost nine times what they had been when Geneen took the helm.

Getty, J. Paul
1892-1976

J. Paul Getty had his father's backing when he began investing in oil leases. He had an uncanny knack of buying land that others had written off and managing to strike it big. His biggest coup was obtaining a sixty-year concession from Saudi Arabia, which eventually made a strike that was colossal. His company was the eighth sister. (The seven sisters were British Petroleum, Royal Dutch Shell, Standard Oil of New Jersey, Standard Oil of California, Mobil, Texaco, and Gulf).

At the age of sixty-four, Getty was America's richest man (Fortune, 1987). His wealth was about $1 billion. Getty lived a fast life. He was married five times. In 1959, he built a sixty acre estate in England and lived there for the rest of his life.

Getty died in 1976 at the age of 83. His company was sold to Texaco for more than $10 billion.

Gianinni, Amadeo Peter
1870-1949

Amadeo Peter Gianinni was the son of an Italian immigrant. He worked in his stepfather's produce firm and became a partner at nineteen. He was well off enough at thirty-one to retire.

He dabbled in real estate and became a director of a bank in 1904. He started the Bank of Italy in a remodeled tavern. By 1918, he had built a chain of twenty-four banks from Santa Rosa to Los Angeles, with $94 million in resources. His main institution in Los Angeles, the Bank of America, had 453 branches in California. By 1929 with assets of more than $1 billion, the Bank of America reached New York with 32 branches.

When stock prices plunged after 1929, his top holding company Transamerica fell from 67 3/8 to a low of 2 and 1/2 in 1932. Gianinni lost his New York bank, but his basic banking organization held firm, and his Bank of America was eventually to become the world's largest.

Gillette, King Camp
1855-1932

In 1901, King C. Gillette and associates formed a company and began operations above a store in South Boston. He had just designed a razor, and told his wife he was going to make a fortune. In 1903 Gillette put his first razor on the market. By the end of the year he sold 51 razors and 168 blades.

Then the new razor caught on, and an international multi-billion dollar business was launched. The company was moved into larger quarters. When we entered World War I, the U.S. Government bought 4.2 million safety razors for servicemen. This was the break that Gillette needed. Gillette's new razor changed the shaving habits of millions of men throughout the world.

In 1948 the Gillette Company started diversifying. It bought the Toni Company which made women's home permanents. In 1955 Gillette added Paper-Mate Ball Point Pens. In the sixties the Right Guard family of deodorants was born. The company employs 1,000 research and technical people. Sales are more than a billion dollars. Another success story in American business is history.

Gimbel Brothers, Inc.

Adam Gimbel founded a business in Vincennes, Indiana in 1842. He landed in America in the mid-nineteenth century. Adam left Bavaria to escape a life of poverty and find an outlet for his ambition in America.

He arrived in New Orleans in 1835 and became a peddler. He loaded a pack with merchandise and traded with Indians, farmers, and backwoodsmen along the banks of the Mississippi. He acquired a horse and wagon, and faced all the hardships of that way of life. In 1842, he bought a building and settled down as the proprietor of a permanent trading post.

Adam Gimbel sold to everyone at the same fixed price. It was revolutionary at that time. On one of his trips to Philadelphia, he met and fell in love with Fridolyn Kahnweiler, the daughter of a dry-goods merchant who was also from Bavaria. Their love affair developed into a marriage and the birth of seven sons-- Jacob, Isaac, Charles, Ellis, Daniel, Louis, and Benedict. They were all trained for employment in the family store.

The years that followed saw expansion to Milwaukee, Wisconsin and Philadelphia. When Adam died, Isaac assumed the presidency. By 1908, Isaac Gimbel was looking at New York City for expansion. Isaac's son Bernard was actively involved with his father in the project. The Herald Square store was built on a site which was rented from the Hudson and Manhattan Railroad for $655,000 a year and was eventually bought for $9,000,000.

Gimbel Brothers became a public company in 1922. The Saks Company was acquired in 1923, for $8,000,000 of Gimbel's stock. One year later Saks opened their store on Fifth Avenue.

The rivalry between Gimbel's and Macy's was a New York tradition, but most of it was good humored and good business. Gimbel's developed thirty-three Gimbel's and Saks main stores and branch stores, throughout the country contributing to a total sales volume of $300,000,000.

Gimbel, Isaac

Isaac Gimbel worked in his father's store until he was 13. With his six brothers he formed Gimbel Brothers chain of stores in Milwaukee (1889), Philadelphia (1894), and New York (1910).

The company expanded with the acquisition of Saks & Company in 1923. Isaac's son Bernard Gimbel was president from 1927 to 1953, when his son Bruce replaced him as president. The company was sold to the Brown and Williamson Tobacco Corporation in 1973, and by 1987 the last Gimbel's store was closed.

Girard, Stephen
1750-1831

Stephen Girard, a one-eyed ship agent from Bordeaux, France got into the wine business and shipping after the revolution. He started with $30,000 from a dissolved partnership with his brother and by 1810 he was able to invest $500,000 of his money in stock of the First Bank of the United States.

Girard lived alone in Philadelphia and was hated and feared by his neighbors. He died in 1831 at the age of 81. He gave his fortune to his relatives, servants, hospitals, and charities. Pennsylvania received $300,000, Philadelphia received $500,000, and the remainder of his $6 million went to found a college for orphans. His estate was $10 million, the largest in America at that time.

Goldman, Marcus
1821-1904

Marcus Goldman was born in Bavaria, near Schweinfurt. He was twenty-seven when he arrived in New York. It was well-known that Jewish immigrants had a peddler's paradise in the coal hills of Pennsylvania. He married a girl from Bavaria from another Goldman family in Philadelphia. They met and fell in love, and were married. Bertha Goldman had a career. She was doing embroidery and needlework for Philadelphia society women. Marcus made the transition from peddler to shopkeeper. He had his own clothing store on Market Street, but Bertha urged him to move to New York.

Marcus hung out a shingle in Pine Street that he was "Marcus Goldman—Banker and Broker." His office was in a cellar next to a coal bin. Goldman carried his business in his hat. He visited the wholesale jewelers in Maiden Lane and the leather merchants in the "swamp." He satisfied these merchants in their need for cash in small amounts at a discount of 8 or 9 percent.

In the afternoon he went uptown to the commercial banks, where he removed his hat and began to dicker. Goldman was doing what the Lehman's did with their cotton bills, what the Seligmans were doing with their bonds. Marcus didn't need a partner. He was able to sell as much as five million dollars worth of commercial paper a year.

Marcus liked to walk and "trade on the street." Walking was a tradition among the Jewish bankers. Jacob Schiff who was preeminent in Wall Street would claim that he made a million dollars while doing his morning constitutional on the deck of the Berengaria. It may be that these "merchant bankers," the Seligmans, Solomon Loeb, and Marcus Goldman were still peddlers, only now they were peddling IOU's.

Goldman, Sol
1917-1987

Sol Goldman was a Brooklyn-born real estate investor who amassed a property fortune estimated to be worth $1 billion.

He started assembling his real estate fortune in the 1930s during the great depression when he was only 17. He and his frequent business partner Alex Di Lorenzo Jr. owned the Chrysler Building and the Stanhope Hotel.

During the high inflation period of the 1970s, the partnership stumbled. In 1975, Di Lorenzo died. They lost the Chrysler Building, and dozens of other properties. But Goldman recovered and began buying again, amassing by some estimates as many as 600 buildings.

Goldman's death in 1987 started a battle over his estate between his estranged wife Lillian and their four children. Lillian died at the age of 82 in 2002.

Goodman, Henry

Henry Goodman was six years old when his father brought him to the United States. It was about the middle of the 19th century, and the family settled in Macon, Georgia. They opened a small dry-goods store.

After the Civil War, the family moved to Lockport, New York, near the Niagara frontier. Henry married Celia Cohn and traveled for the family's business, the Superba Cravat Company of Rochester, New York. Henry and Celia lived in Rochester, where their son Edwin, the founder of the New York business, grew up . Edwin worked on a tailor's bench at the Stein-Bloch factory in Rochester.

Edwin's first job was at a shop on Sixth Avenue. He soon learned about a small tailoring shop at 125 Fifth Avenue, Bergdorf & Voigt, where single and double breasted suits were adapted to the female form. Herman Bergdorf was a Frenchman from Alsace. He liked hard work and drinking wine. Edwin Goodman was 23 when he came to Bergdorf in 1899. Edwin met Belle Lowenstein at Bergdorf's. Her father did not approve of Edwin, so Edwin used capital provided by the Cohn family, and in 1901 Bergdorf Goodman was born. Belle Lowenstein's father gave his blessing to the union of his daughter to Edwin, and their wedding took place in 1903.

Eventually, Bergdorf sold his share of the business to Edwin for $15,000 and retired to Paris. Edwin Goodman died in 1953, half a century after he bought out Herman Bergdorf. An annual business volume of $20 million is merely a milestone in a story of continuing success.

Goodrich, Dr. Benjamin Franklin
1841-1888

Dr. B.F. Goodrich died at the age of forty-six. He overcame poverty and poor health to become an Army surgeon during the Civil War and a pioneering businessman.

Goodrich loaned his support to the Hudson River Rubber Company in 1868. He was certain that rubber had a future, although Hudson River was failing. He moved west to Akron, Ohio, and on December 31, 1870, a new factory was turning out many products including a cotton-covered rubber hose. Success was still a dream.

Alexander Winton, a bicycle manufacturer, wanted pneumatic tires made for a horseless carriage he had invented. Goodrich said, "I guess we can make them, although we never have." The rest is history. The B.F. Goodrich Company produced the tires for the first gasoline-powered car in the United States.

B.F. Goodrich is one of America's largest corporations. Its research has led to vulcanized rubber, carbon black use in tires, and vinyl. Dr. Goodrich raised the standards of the entire rubber industry, which contributes materially to our economic and social progress.

Goodyear, Charles
1800-1860

Charles Goodyear developed vulcanized rubber, used in tire manufacturing. It made his name a household word to this day. His wonderful invention was pirated by many manufacturing giants.

Goodyear engaged in protracted litigation which only succeeded in driving himself into bankruptcy. "He died loaded down with debt, and a broken-down man," said Gustavus Myers. He was only sixty years old.

The Goodyear Blimp is a common sight and the Goodyear Tire Company is still one of the major tire manufacturing companies.

Gould, Jay
1836-1892

The story of Jay Gould is so fantastic that it exceeds the bounds of fiction. Born in upstate New York, the son of a poor farmer, Gould rose to prominence in the railroad business. His modus operandi was to buy two bad roads, merge them under a new name, and float bonds at a good price. He would sell the new road to a buyer at a large profit, and if the new owner could not make a profit after a year or two he'd buy back the road at greatly reduced prices.

Jay Gould's accomplishments are so numerous that it would take a book to list them. He was called "the little wizard." Daniel Drew said, "His look was death!" Gould was described by someone as "A person who did not get up early in the morning, he stayed up all night."

Gould outsmarted his adversaries and amassed a total of $70 million dollars. His holdings included railroads, Western Union, and New York's elevated lines. However, Gould will forever be remembered for his attempt to corner the gold market in 1869 with Jim Fisk. In the most daring display of financial acumen, Gould and Fisk forced the price of gold to new highs in an effort to corner the shorts. They were assured by Abel Corbin, President Grant's brother-in-law that the government would hold off sales from the treasury. The corner was broken when Grant released gold for sale. It was one of the most dramatic moments in the history of speculation. Black Friday was September 24, 1869. Gould had ridden out the storm in safety. It was determined in a later investigation that he had sold all his gold on September 24th at its crest in the morning, and made millions in one of the greatest coups of his career.

Gould was a loner. He died prematurely of consumption in 1892. He bought Union Pacific $100 par at $50 and even as low as 14 after the Credit Mobilier Scandal. He took control, propped it up, and made $20 million out of it. Gould controlled Western Union, the Rapid Transit Lines of New York City, and the New York World. He acquired many defunct roads, franchises, and land grants. He also owned The Pacific Mail Steamship Company in partnership with Collis Huntington.

The closest Gould came to defeat was during the Grant and Ward Panic of 1884. Every enterprise he owned was battered down to bankruptcy levels. Was Jay Gould beaten? Not quite. He threatened his enemies that he would go bankrupt and that would cause a universal crash that would bring them down. They let up on him with terms of receiving 50,000 Western Union shares at 50 which they had sold much higher. They expected him to fail soon after. But Gould used the money they released to corner Missouri Pacific and other stocks in which his enemies were trapped. He escaped miraculously, as usual, without suffering the inevitable failure. He died in 1892 while still bent upon new campaigns of conquest.

Grace, W.R.
1832-1904

William Russell Grace was a pioneer who turned Guano (bird droppings) into one of the world's largest corporations. Grace became influential in Peru and helped reorganize the country's finances. In return, he acquired the silver and copper mines of Cerro de Pasco, 5 million acres of oil and mineral-rich lands, sixty-six year leases on the railroads, and grants to Peru's supply of Guano.

Grace was an immigrant from the potato famine in Ireland. He was elected Mayor of New York City in 1880 and reelected in 1884. W.R. Grace has annual sales of over $2 billion dollars.

Graham, Benjamin
1894-1976

Benjamin Graham is considered the father of fundamental analysis. Experience taught Graham the valuable lessons which developed into his investment principles. He advocates four main steps in the selection of a portfolio:

- Adequate diversification.
- Buy large, prominent, conservatively financed companies.
- They should have a record of continuous dividend payment.
- They should have a reasonably low price-earnings ratio.

Graham insists that you should not enter an operation unless your calculation shows it has a fair chance of showing a reasonable profit. Have the courage of your knowledge and experience. Above all, be guided by Graham's tenet that investments should be based on arithmetic, not optimism.

He bans the purchase of all stocks that sell over twenty-five times earnings. This effectively excludes all growth stocks. He feels that value will out. Graham is partial to closed-end funds since they can be bought at a 20 percent discount.

Graham's concepts cannot be overemphasized. It is important to note that Graham was the mentor for Warren Buffett, "the Sage of Omaha." His following Graham's ideas helped him become one of the richest men in the world.

Graham was born "Grossbaum."

Greeley, Horace
1817-1872

Horace Greeley was one of America's most influential newspaper editors. He was editor of the New York Tribune. He is known for his statement, "Go to the west."

Greeley stated that in America, status and education were not prerequisites for success. He cited John Jacob Astor and Cornelius Vanderbilt as examples. Astor was an orphan and Vanderbilt started his career with one sailboat.

Greeley was positive about America. He said, "Americans are energetic, we are audacious, and we are confident in our capacities and in our national destiny."

Green, Hetty Robinson
1834-1916

Hetty Green was a 19th century shipping heiress who ran a fortune of a few million dollars into more than one hundred million in a forty year period.

Green once threatened the notoriously ruthless Collis P. Huntington with a revolver when she thought he was cheating her in a deal. She stands alone as an American woman of unquestioned financial genius and achieved this standing at the cost of being generally considered a witch.

Hetty Green was called, "The Witch of Wall Street."

Greenberg, Maurice Raymond (Hank)
1925-

Maurice "Hank" Greenberg was made head of AIG in 1962. He held that position until 2005. Greenberg is the son of Jacob Greenberg, a candy store owner. After his father died, his mother married a dairy farmer.

Greenberg served in the U.S. Army during World War II, and participated in the liberation of Dachau. He was awarded the Bronze Star and rose to the rank of Captain. He also served in the Korean War.

Greenberg attended the University of Miami and New York Law School. He has several honorary degrees. He is married and has four children, three sons and one daughter. Together, he and his sons controlled a major portion of the insurance industry.

During Greenberg's tenure at the helm of American International Group (AIG), the company developed into the 18th largest public company and the largest insurance and financial services corporation.

Guggenheim, Isaac
Year Uncertain- 1807

Isaac Guggenheim was the patriarch of the Guggenheim family. He died in 1807.
He amassed a fortune as a money-lender-25,000 Florins. His oldest son, Meyer had eight children, four boys and four girls. Samuel was making a name for himself. He saved two children from a fire in 1818.

In 1848, when Simon was in his fifties he married a fifty-one year old widow Rachel. Meyer had seven children, three sons and four daughters. The combined families, fourteen in all set off for America in 1847. Two months later they landed in Philadelphia. Simon was 56, his son Meyer was 20. They set off peddling in coal country, as the Seligmans had done a decade before. A shipboard romance resulted in the marriage of Meyer and his fifteen- year-old stepsister Barbara in 1852.

Meyer found that for every dollar's worth of goods, he was returning sixty to seventy cents to the manufacturer. This caused Meyer to develop a stove polish he could manufacture. Meyer sold his stove polish and lye company for $150,000. He made money in the stock market and his wife wanted to leave Philadelphia and move to New York.

Meyer was rich but he had not reached his goal. A friend, Charles H. Graham came to talk to Meyer about some mining shares. More likely, Graham owed Meyer some money and persuaded him to accept mining shares in lieu of cash. Meyer became a one-third owner of two lead and silver mines called the "A.Y." and "The Minnie," outside of Leadville, Colorado. Meyer went to Leadville to inspect his holdings and promptly pumped out the mines. After he almost gave up, he was told that he had a rich strike. Meyer learned that the real money to be made was in smelting and refining. The result was the founding of The American Smelting and Refining Company, which made the Guggenheim's fortune as large as the Rockefeller's.

Guggenheim, Meyer
1826-1905

Meyer Guggenheim, a Swiss immigrant, was eking out a living as a peddler. He made a penny on a ten cent sale of shoe polish. He learned that the maker earned seven cents on the same can. He put his family to work making the polish. He did the same thing with a lye for soap making. He made a modest fortune.

Meyer Guggenheim made $300,000 in a railroad stock following Jay Gould. Eventually, he owned a couple of Colorado silver mines. He was impressed with the larger profits made by the smelter. In 1889, The Guggenheim's built their own smelter and by 1895, the family holdings were producing profits of $1,000,000 a year.

In 1900, The Guggenheim's sold all their smelting interests and most of their other properties for $425 million in stock of American Smelting and Refining. It was enough to control the company. Soon the Guggenheim interests controlled another smelting combination organized by Morgan called The Kennecott Copper Corporation.

Halliburton, Erle Palmer
1892-1957

Erle Halliburton was an American businessman specializing in the oil business. After his service in the Navy, Halliburton headed for the oil fields of California. His drive and innovation led to his getting hired and fired. He has commented that it was the best thing that could have happened to him.

He moved to Oklahoma where he invented, perfected, and patented a new method of oil well cementing. By 1922, his company was called the Halliburton Oil Well Cementing Company. On July 5, 1911 it became known as the Halliburton Company.

Hamilton, Alexander
1755 or 1757- 1804

Hamilton was born in Nevis in the British West Indies. He was apprenticed to a merchant at St. Croix. The owner died, and at the age of fifteen young Hamilton took full control of the trading house and ran it very well.

Hamilton enrolled at Princeton at the age of sixteen. When he couldn't proceed at his own pace he left Princeton and went to King's College (now Columbia) which agreed with his stipulations.

During the war he attracted George Washington's attention. He rose to the rank of Lieutenant Colonel and he became Washington's secretary. Hamilton married into the wealthy Schuyler family and went into politics.

When the delegates gathered in Philadelphia, the nation was hoping they could bring forth a better system of government. Thomas Jefferson believed in the preservation of states' rights. Hamilton favored a strong central government.

Hamilton became Secretary of the Treasury in 1789. We owed $12 million to France, Holland, and Spain. All other debts amounted to $77 million. Hamilton wanted to pay off the debt. He encountered opposition from the states. Eventually, a Tariff Bill was passed, and America was on its way to becoming the manufacturing giant that it is today. In 1791, The First Bank of the United States was chartered for twenty years.

Hamilton, William Peter
1867-1929

William Peter Hamilton was one of the most important individuals who refined and developed the Dow Theory. He felt that there were definite reasons for market movement. He was certain that the Dow Theory can predict fairly accurately, that movement.

He believed that the stock market is the barometer of the country's business. From the 1900s to his death in 1929, Hamilton studied, explained, developed, and asserted the Dow Theory to provide a foundation on which technical analysis would thrive.

Hamilton's record of forecasting was impressive. He predicted the Panic of 1907, the bear market of 1917, and six major bull and bear markets. He also gave a bearish warning right before the crash of 1929.

Hamilton was born in England in 1867. At the age of 32 he came to New York and joined The Wall Street Journal. He become editor of the editorial page nine years later and held that post until he died at the age of 63.

Hamilton revised the Dow Theory, claiming that the railroad and industrial average must corroborate each other before any prediction for a change in the direction of the market can be given.

Hammer, Armand
1898-1990

Armand Hammer was born in Manhattan, New York. His parents were Russian-born immigrants. His father came to the United States in 1875 from Odessa (Ukraine). He lived in the Bronx where he had a general medical practice and five drug stores.

Armand's father was a Socialist and had a leadership role in the Socialist Labor Party (SLP) which was a founding element of the Communist Party. Hammer confirmed that the origin of his name was the "Arm and Hammer" which was the symbol of the Socialist Labor Party. Julius Hammer served two and a half years in Sing Sing prison for performing an abortion on a woman with pneumonia who subsequently died.

Hammer received an M.D. degree from Columbia Medical School in 1921. His first business success was selling a ginger extract laced with alcohol during prohibition, which had $1 million in sales. Prior to his internship at Bellevue Hospital, Hammer went to the Soviet Union. He stayed there for nine years, until 1930. A skeptical U.S. government watched Hammer during this trip and for the rest of his life.

After returning to the U.S., Hammer began investing in oil. These investments eventually developed into control of Occidental Petroleum. Hammer was a staunch Republican and donated $54,000 to the campaign of Richard Nixon in 1986. Forbes Magazine estimated his net worth at $200 million.

There have been five biographies and two autobiographies of this remarkable man. He was a philanthropist, art collector, and the winner of numerous distinguished awards from nations all over the world. The only award he never won was the Nobel Peace Prize.

Hancock, John
1736-1793

John Hancock is known for his signature on the Declaration of Independence. It denotes his large ego. He inherited a very successful business from his uncle who was one of the wealthiest merchants in New England.

Hancock was born in Braintree, Massachusetts in 1736. He lived with his uncle after his father died. Thomas Hancock had no children. He had a book-selling and publishing business in Boston. Thomas adopted his nephew John and sent him to Harvard. When his uncle died in 1754, John became the head of the largest and most profitable mercantile houses in Boston. He was 27. By 1775, the firm went out of business due mainly to the declining relationship of Britain to the colonies.

Hancock became active in politics and was elected President of the Continental Congress. He was expected to be named Commander-in-Chief of the Continental Army but he was not the equal of George Washington. He was elected nine times as Governor of Massachusetts. John Hancock died in office in 1793, leaving a fortune of $350,000.

Harriman, Edward Henry (Ned)
1848-1909

A shy quiet man who looked like a bookkeeper and operated like a tycoon, Edward Harriman was the son of a minister. He sold short during Jay Gould's Black Friday raid in 1869. He made $3,000 and bought a stock exchange seat when he was just twenty-one. His clients were August Belmont, the Vanderbilt's, and Jay Gould.

In 1879 he married the daughter of William J. Averill, a part-owner of a small railroad in Ogdensburg, New York. This led to various deals and finally control of Illinois Central. Harriman was fearless and took on Morgan. Morgan respected him.

Harriman made the Union Pacific a money-maker. The next acquisition was the Southern Pacific. In a bid to rival J.P. Morgan, Harriman bought control of several insurance companies in 1908. We will never know how rich Edward Harriman could have grown. He could have owned all the railroads in the country. He became ill in 1909 and died. He is no doubt one of the outstanding railroad moguls of the post Civil War period

J.P. Morgan had few defeats in his career, but Edward H. Harriman bested him in Dubuque and Sioux City. Morgan fumed over the defeat and would never forgive "that little fellow." Both men were ambitious. Harriman planned something that everyone said was impossible. He would then "jump in with both feet and do it!" Harriman was the son of a disappointed minister who was born in Hempstead in 1848. He was quite a boy on Wall Street, and he gathered a thorough education in capitalism. He watched Commodore Vanderbilt, Jay Gould and the lonely wizard James R. Keene (The Silver Fox) with corners and pools. Harriman was a bear by disposition.

Harriman was brilliantly deceptive, impassive, laconic, quick-thinking, and calculating. He demanded the respect of his peers.

Harriman's reputation was unpleasant. He was a cold-blooded gambler like Jay Gould. It would stick to him all his life. He turned defeat into victory in the dissolution of the Northern Securities Corporation. His Union Pacific Group had a windfall of $58 million. He or his agents became the directors of the Baltimore and Ohio, Northern Pacific, Atchison, Topeka, and Santa Fe, Illinois Central, and the New York Central. Harriman feared neither God nor Morgan. He reigned as a Napoleon of the railways during a brief and meteoric career that ended suddenly by his complete exhaustion and early death. It was said that if he had lived he would have probably owned all the railroads in the country.

Hartford, George Huntington II
1911-2008

George Huntington Hartford II was an American businessman, philanthropist, filmmaker, and art collector. He was the heir to the A & P supermarket fortune. He owned Paradise Island in the Bahamas and the Oil Shale Corporation (Tosco). On his death in 2008, numerous obituaries stated that "he had once ranked among the world's richest people."

Huntington's father, Edward V. Hartford (1870-1922) died when Huntington was eleven, leaving his son as the heir to the estate left by his grandfather, George Huntington Hartford. Huntington graduated from Harvard in 1934. For the rest of his life he focused on various business and charitable enterprises. He was married four times and had four children. He lived the last years of his life in the Bahamas.

Huntington lived on a trust fund that generated $1.5 million per year. In 1940, Huntington invested $100,000 to help start a newspaper, PM. He was an avid sailor, and he donated his yacht to the Coast Guard at the start of the war. He settled in Los Angeles, California where he tried to buy Republic Pictures and RKO Studios from Howard Hughes.

In 1969, he was worth half a billion dollars. Huntington's grandfather and his uncle privately owned the A & P supermarket chain, which at one point had 16,000 stores in the U.S. It was the largest retail empire in the world.

Harvey, Fred Henry
1835-1901

Fred Harvey was born in London and immigrated to the United States at the age of 15. He worked as a pot scrubber in New York City. He saved his money and opened his own restaurant. His partner gave up on the restaurant, took the money, and left town.

In 1875, Harvey opened two restaurants along a railroad route. He then offered the Atchison, Topeka, and Santa Fe Railroad a plan to provide high quality eating places with good food, reasonable prices, and efficient service. The deal was approved with a handshake. At the age of 41, Fred Harvey had finally established a successful restaurant.

By 1883, Harvey had a chain of 17 "Harvey Houses" scattered along the Atchison, Topeka, and Santa Fe line. Some food critics proclaimed that the fare at the Harvey Houses was the best in the land. The chain proved so profitable that the Atchison, Topeka, and Santa Fe reviewed its deal with Harvey in 1889. In 1900, with his health failing, Harvey turned over his business empire of 47 restaurants, 30 dining cars, 15 hotels, etc. to his sons and sons-in-law. He died a few months later, on February 9, 1901.

Hearst, George
1820-1891

George Hearst was one of the richest men in the history of American mining. He was twenty-eight when gold was discovered in California. In 1850 he set off for the mines. For $10,000 he bought part of the Comstock Lode.

In 1876, he paid $80,000 for a gold mine property in South Dakota's Black Hills. He called it Homestake Mining. It became the mainstay of his fortune and has paid more than $160 million in dividends.

At one time he bought 1,000,000 acres in Mexico for forty cents an acre. In California, he paid seventy cents an acre for a 40,000 acre ranch that ran from the mountains to the ocean. In 1880, he bought the San Francisco Examiner. His son, William Randolph Hearst used it to embark on his career as the builder of a great newspaper and magazine empire.

Hearst, William Randolph
1863-1951

William Randolph Hearst was one of the biggest spenders in American history. He spent about $15 million every year. Hearst built the fantastic mansion San Simeon in California. The pool alone cost $1 million. He owned seven castles around the world. He enjoyed his money.

Despite his attempt to deplete his fortune, Hearst still had more than $59 million when he died in 1951 at the age of eighty-eight. In 1995, the family trust had reached a value of more than $45 million according to Forbes' estimates.

Citizen Kane, a movie with Orson Welles, depicts the life of William Randolph Hearst. It is one of the greatest movies of all time.

Hefner, Hugh
1926-

Hugh Hefner was born in Chicago. He transformed the entertainment industry with the publication of Playboy Magazine. He featured Marilyn Monroe in 1953. He expanded his empire with television and web ventures.

Hefner served two years in the U.S. Army in World War II. He earned a bachelor's degree from the University of Illinois at Urbana. He started with an entry-level job at Esquire. He left quickly because he was denied a five dollar raise. He raised $5,000 from 45 investors and launched Playboy.

The first issue sold 50,000 copies and became an instant sensation. The magazine was a welcome antidote to 30 years of war and depression.

Heinz, H.J.
1844-1919

Henry J. Heinz raised horseradish in his family's small garden while he was still a boy. He began grating it in vinegar and selling it to his neighbors. This began his journey, and his life's work. After starting his business with his two brothers, within six years Heinz was selling more than 6,000 barrels a year of sauerkraut, celery sauce, vinegar, and pickles. Tomato ketchup appeared in 1879. New products were added and the famous "57 varieties" slogan was dreamed up by Heinz in 1896.

In 1919, the year of his death, Heinz's company had more than 6,000 employees in twenty-five U.S. and overseas plants.

Hill, James Jerome
1838-1916

James J. Hill was a Canadian. He was an American stock market operator. He was a pioneer railroad man and father of the Great Northern Railway that opened up the Pacific Northwest.

The one-eyed, heavy-set Canadian had built up the Great Northern by helping to develop the territory it covered. He brought in settlers, promoted industries, drained the land, pushed crop diversification, and improved the strain of cattle. When hard times sent other roads into bankruptcy, he remained solvent.

When the Northern Pacific went under in 1894, Hill tried to gain control of a rival line. He joined with J.P. Morgan and bought enough stock in the open market to gain control. Hill raised money by selling land. Masses of Norwegian and Swedish peasants produced 32 million bushels of wheat. It saved Hill and caused the earnings of his road to triple. Jim Hill was short and thick-set. He had a massive head, long black hair, wrinkled features and a blind eye. He carried everything in his head, worried, and drove himself and others. He had no scruples, and was despotic and intolerant of opposition. He ruled by fear and was also given to personal violence.

Hill sought large volume by giving low rates to beat his competition. He was an able administrator, buying shrewdly, ruthlessly hiring and firing. He sent agents to Europe with stereopticon slides to bring immigrants by the hundred thousand at low fares into his domain. He undermined the reviving Northern Pacific with low rates. He founded schools, churches, and whole communities. He encouraged cattle- raising and tree -planting. In short, he built the Northwest section of the United States as if it were his own. The west coast over the Rockies beckoned. His dream was to reach Seattle, Tacoma, and Portland on the Pacific.

Hollerith, Herman
1860-1929

Herman Hollerith received an engineering degree from Columbia University. He helped one of his professors for the 1880 National Census in Washington, D.C. It took seven years to tabulate.

A suggestion by someone that there should be a better way to do such painstaking work led Hollerith to draw his inspiration from a conductor who punched holes in a railroad ticket. He built a pantographic punch that could record an individual's vital statistics by means of holes in a card, which could be read with the help of electromagnets. The 1890 census took only three years and Hollerith's device saved almost $5 million.

Hollerith formed the Tabulating Machines Company, which proved to be the forerunner of the great International Business Machines.

Hopkins, Johns
1796-1873

The growth of Baltimore, Maryland is a direct result of Johns Hopkins'
financial aid. Baltimore grew from a population of 35,000 in 1800 to America's third largest city, with a population of more than 300,000.

At 17, Hopkins joined his uncle's wholesale grocery. He fell in love with his cousin Elizabeth, but his uncle forbade their marriage. They remained friends and neither of them married. It led to a falling out between Hopkins and his uncle.

Hopkins' business built a $10 million fortune. He gave most of it away. He dealt in whiskey, and later into hard goods and banking. He also invested in property in Baltimore and other areas. His most important investment was the Baltimore & Ohio Railroad. During the Panic of 1873, he loaned the railroad $900,000 to carry it through the crisis.

Hopkins loaned the city of Baltimore $500,000 to take it through the Civil War. After making provisions for his family, Hopkins left the bulk of his fortune to charity. His $7 million founded Johns Hopkins University Medical School and Johns Hopkins Hospital. It was the largest philanthropic bequest in U.S. history. Johns Hopkins will always be remembered by the school that bears his name. It is one of the world's leading universities.

Hopkins, Mark
1813-1878

Mark Hopkins is the second member of the big four to open a new store—the Huntington and Hopkins hardware store. It became one of the most prosperous retail-wholesale firms in California. Through their involvement in city politics they met their future partners Leland Stanford and Charles Crocker.

The four partners built the Central Pacific and met the Union Pacific in Utah where the Golden Spike was hammered home. The government paid the big four $16,000 for every mile of track across the flat lands, and $48,000 for every mile across the mountains. All told, the partners were given $25 million in government bonds and 4.5 million acres of land.

The railroad was financed by the government, but the partners kept the profits. When congress requested the company's books, they were "accidentally" lost in a fire. The next project was the Southern Pacific. By 1884, the Southern Pacific stretched from the west coast to New Orleans. The big four had already built Reno, Nevada, Fresno, California, and other towns along the route. The partners became the largest landlord in California, Utah, and Nevada. They controlled 3.8 million acres.

Hughes, Howard
1905-1976

Howard Hughes inherited the Hughes Tool Company that his father founded. Howard's father invented a superior tool bit to drill for oil and it led to the fortune that Howard Hughes used as the core of his investment funds.

Hughes liked the movies and aviation. In 1948, he bought RKO and after seven years he sold out and made $1 million profit. In 1932, he founded Hughes Aircraft. It went nowhere. He bought an airline in 1937 and named it Trans World Airways. He sold his 78 percent share for $546 million.

He built the largest plane in the world, "The Spruce Goose." It was an eight-engine flying boat that could hold seven hundred people. It was only able to fly one mile before it was put into mothballs.

In the 1950s, Hughes disappeared in Las Vegas hotels and then to the Bahamas, London, Managua, and Acapulco. His fortune was about $14 billion, but when he died in 1976 he left only $600 million to $900 million. After his death, Hughes Aircraft was sold to General Motors for $5.2 billion. Howard Hughes was an eccentric Croesus who clung to the shadowy background while his lucrative enterprises piled up millions in the foreground.

Hunt, Haroldson Lafayette (H.L.)
1889-1974

H.L. Hunt bought out G.M. "Dad" Joiner, and 5,000 acres of land in East Texas which began his rise to a fortune. It cost him only $30,000 in cash up front. It turned out to be one of the biggest oil-producing fields in East Texas.

Hunt was one of eight children of an Illinois cattle farmer. He started with a $6,000 inheritance from his father. In 1923, at the age of 34, Hunt owned 44 oil wells in Arkansas. One year later he sold a half-interest in 40 wells for $600,000. He then went to Texas and founded the Hunt Oil Company in 1936. His 60,000 barrels a day were netting him $1,000,000 every week. Hunt was shy and soft-spoken. He looked like Herbert Hoover.

Hunt had a complex personal life. He had fourteen children with three women. Two of his sons from his first wife, Bunker and Herbert lost most of their fortune in their attempt to corner the silver market. J. Paul Getty once conceded saying," In terms of extraordinary wealth, there is only one man---H.L. Hunt."

Huntington, Collis Potter
1821-1900

Collis Huntington was the son of a Connecticut tinker who was so poor he sent Collis to live with local farmers. He worked as a peddler before opening a store with his brother in Oneonta, New York. The gold rush brought Collis to California to open a store there. He set up a store in Sacramento. Mark Hopkins became his partner. Their involvement in city politics was how they met the other two members of the big four who were so powerful in California's history—Charles Crocker and Leland Stanford.

Huntington ended up the wealthiest of the big four. He had a fortune estimated at between $60 and $70 million before he died at the age of 79. He gained control of the Chesapeake and Ohio Railroad. He extended that line to Huntington, West Virginia, and he also built the town of Newport News, Virginia.

Huntington was married twice and adopted two children, but his business interests were passed on to his brother's son Henry E. Huntington, then fifty, who received one third of his uncle's shares in Southern Pacific.

Icahn, Carl Celian
1936-

Carl Icahn is an American business magnate. He was born in Far Rockaway, Queens, New York City. He graduated from Far Rockaway High School and received a BA degree from Princeton in 1968. He attended N.Y.U. School of Medicine but left without graduating.

Icahn began his career in Wall Street in 1961. Many people believe that he began taking positions in individual companies using "junk bonds" and "mortgage bonds" in the period that transformed corporate America. He developed a reputation as a ruthless corporate raider with a hostile takeover of TWA in 1986. He launched a $7 billion move on U.S. Steel but was rebuffed by CEO David Roderick.

In 2007, Icahn and his affiliates owned majority positions in many firms. He owned billions of dollars of Time Warner and made an attempt to increase shareholder value. Icahn tried to acquire Marvel Comics, but it was bought by The Walt Disney Company in 2009. He owns 5.6 percent of Biogen Idec and is continuing to add to his position. On December 31, 2012 Icahn acquired a 10% position in Netflix.

Other companies which Icahn has been involved with are Motorola, Yahoo, Hain Celestial, The Clorox Company, Mentor Graphics, Lions Gate Films, and Imclone. His career has seen its share of poison pills. Greenmail, and proxy battles.

Ingram, Billy and Anderson, Walter

Billy Ingram and Walter Anderson changed the eating habits in the United States. They were pioneers in the fast food industry. Their White Castle restaurant chain served more hamburgers than any other restaurant chain in the world. In 1937, White Castle served 40 million hamburgers.

While the growth of White Castle has been eclipsed by McDonald's, Burger King, and Wendy's, Anderson and Ingram achieved the feat of taking a little-known and poorly regarded hamburger and making it acceptable and even desirable.

Insull, Samuel
1859-1938

Samuel Insull, son of a poor London clergyman, was a great admirer of Thomas Edison. He answered a newspaper ad and eventually became Edison's secretary. He moved up rapidly in the Edison organization and became President of the Edison Power Company in Chicago when he was still in his thirties.

As the years went by, Insull Utility Investments, Inc. controlled by his family and his banker, Halsey, Stuart & Co. served 45 million customers. His systems produced 10 percent of the nation's electric power in 1930, and had assets valued at $2.5 billion.

After the crash, stock prices continued to drop, and Insull could no longer cover his loans. The banks took over the collateral and got control of the Insull companies, forcing Insull to resign. In April, 1932, a petition was filed asking that Insull's top holding companies be put into receivership, triggering one of the biggest failures in U.S. history. Losses ran more than $700 million.

Insull fled the country, but he was brought back from Turkey to face his accusers. He was acquitted, and the proceedings brought out the facts that helped raise him in public esteem. While his own financial empire had collapsed, not one of his operating companies had failed.

Jerome, Addison G.

Jerome Addison was a bull through 1856 and 1857. However, he came out of the 1857 Panic with his health and capital shattered. By 1860, he had laid the foundation for the future. He was one of the few men who bought heavily when share prices were at their lowest ebb. He made fortunes when there was news of a defeat of the Union forces. Jerome was always in the market as a buyer. Addison coined money by the hundreds of thousands through these tactics. He was now worth millions.

A Michigan Southern debacle lost him a million. Shortly thereafter, he died from heart trouble, but he left a rare name in Wall Street. He was never known to allow an oath, a lie, or a vulgar jest to pass his lips. This is an immortal eulogy.

Jerome. Leonard W.
1817-1891

Leonard Jerome graduated from Princeton and President Millard Fillmore took a liking to him and the result was a consular appointment to Italy. His eldest brother Addison G. proposed that they form a partnership before he could leave for Paris. The firm Fitch, McNeal & Jerome went to the wall upon his arrival in New York. He formed a partnership with William R. Travers in 1856. Leonard was a bear, and used the press to demoralize investors. He made a great deal of money, dissolved his partnership, and sailed for Europe on a two year vacation.

After his return, Leonard concentrated on Pacific Mail Steamship Company. He took the stock from 62 to 329 in 1865. He realized enormous sums of money. He spent money freely. He bought a yacht, gave dinner parties where he gave lady guests lavish gifts, and he founded The Jockey Club-a private theatre of his own.

In the end, Pacific Mail, the stock that made his fortune was the cause of his destruction. It melted away all of his money, and he was crippled beyond hope. He then left Wall Street and went to Paris where he lived in retirement.

Leonard Jerome was the grandfather of Winston Churchill.

Jobs, Steve
1955-2011

Steve Jobs and Steve Wozniak started Apple in his parents' garage when he was twenty. They worked hard and in just two years Apple was a $2 billion dollar company employing over four thousand people.

At thirty, Jobs got fired. He had hired someone to run the company and eventually they had a falling out. The Board of Directors sided with the new CEO, and Jobs was out. It was devastating! As it so often happens, getting fired was the best thing that could have happened to Steve Jobs. It freed him to enter the most creative period of his life.

This amazing man started a company named Next, another named Pixar, and fell in love with an amazing woman. They married and have a wonderful family. Job was rehired by Apple and in the years that followed, Jobs developed the I-pod, I-tunes, I-phones, and the I-pad. Apple went from a floundering company, losing 1 billion a year to one of the world's most valuable corporations with $100 billion dollars in revenues.

Then one morning Jobs was diagnosed with Pancreatic Cancer. His doctor said that it was incurable and that he had no longer than three to six months to live. It turned out that surgery was possible, so Jobs had the surgery and was fine, for a while.

No one wants to die, but we all have to face the inevitable. Steve Jobs did. But while we all must die, not everyone really lives---Steve Jobs did.

Johnson, Robert Wood Jr.
1893-1968

Robert Johnson Jr. was a Brigadier General after his service in World War II. His father, Robert Wood Johnson Sr. was a pharmacist who developed antiseptic bandages. He applied the teachings of Joseph Lister who advocated antiseptic surgery and protecting the wounds to prevent infection.

Robert Wood Johnson Jr. was born near New Brunswick, New Jersey where Johnson & Johnson has its headquarters. When he took the helm of the company it had sales of $11 million per year. He expanded the product line and geographic reach to 120 countries. When he died, the company was the world's largest manufacturer of surgical dressings, medical aids, and baby products. It had annual sales of $750 million. The Robert Wood Foundation was given $1 billion in J & J stock. Johnson was survived by his widow and two children.

His brother, John Seward left an estate to his widow and six children that would grow to $1.6 billion in 1995. By 1990, Johnson & Johnson had grown to more than $9 billion in sales with more than 82,000 employees.

Jonsson J. Erik
1901-1995

Geophysical Services, Inc. offered John Erik Jonsson a job running its manufacturing of instruments. Jonsson proved to be the genius of G.S.I. and a prophet who saw the application of electronic products for the military.

When the transistor was first demonstrated in 1948, Jonsson was interested. Texas instruments sent a $25,000 check.

In 1954, Texas Instruments scientists built transistors from silicon and gave the company a lead on the competition. Sales climbed rapidly from $28.7 million in 1955 to $193 million in 1959. By the 1970s the company moved into the list of the top 200 industrial firms in the United States and had sales of well over $800 million.

Kahn, Otto Hermann
1867-1934

Otto Kahn grew up in Mannheim. He went to London in 1888, where he became a British subject, and worked for Deutsche Bank. At the invitation of Speyer & Company he came to New York in 1893. He was twenty-seven. There he met Abe Wolff's daughter Addie. In 1896, he joined Kuhn, Loeb & Company by marrying a partner's daughter

Kahn befriended E.H. Harriman and got along with him better than Jacob Schiff did. He was the bank's chief liason with Harriman. Like his friend Felix Warburg, Otto Kahn was a glamorous person. He was sartorially splendid. Through Kahn, the city's Jewish and Gentile elite embarked on a new relationship. He became a member of the Board of the Metropolitan Opera and proceeded to buy shares until he virtually owned the Metropolitan Opera. He brought Enrico Caruso and Arturo Toscanini to the Met. Kahn was a man about town- a fashion plate. He could also speak with "a beautiful English accent." He was in demand as a public speaker. He loved the spotlight. He loved the press and they loved him. In 1932, Kahn revealed that his gifts to the Metropolitan Opera amounted to over two million dollars.

In the 1930s Kahn dropped his plan to convert to Roman Catholicism and called for all Jews to stand together in light of what Hitler was doing. In the winter of 1934, Otto Kahn went to Palm Beach, as usual, and returned at the end of March. On March 29th he went to his office, and rising from luncheon in the Kuhn, Loeb private dining room, he fell forward, dead.

Kaiser, Henry John
1882-1967

Henry Kaiser was an American industrialist who became known as the father of modern American shipbuilding. He established the Kaiser shipyard which built Liberty Ships during World War II. He later formed Kaiser Aluminum, Kaiser Steel, and organized Kaiser Permanente Health Care for his workers and their families. He led Kaiser-Frazer Automobile companies, known for the safety of their designs.

Kaiser was born in Sprout Brook, New York, near Canajoharie. He was a photographer, and then moved to Washington State where he started a construction company. He built roads, dams, bridges, etc. He was one of the prime contractors in building the Hoover Dam on the Colorado River and the Bonneville and Grand Coulee Dams on the Columbia River.

He never built a ship before, but he set up shipyards in Seattle and Tacoma using a mass-production technique with welding instead of rivets. This created an unprecedented assembly line whereby ships could be constructed in less than five days. The concepts he developed for the mass production of commercial and military ships remain in use today.

Keene, James R.
1838-1913

James R. Keene, "The Silver Fox," is known for his handling the distribution of J.P. Morgan's United States Steel in 1901. His fee was a million dollars in cash and a percentage of the syndicate's profits.

These profits were reported as amounting to $40,000,000, or 20 percent of the syndicate's commitments, of which only one-eighth, or $25,000,000, was paid in.

Keep, Henry
1863-1905

Henry Keep was born in a poorhouse. He was named, "Henry the Silent." At nineteen he left a rival apprenticeship, and ran away to Rochester. He became a bootblack and porter of a hotel. Keep saved his money and with a few thousand dollars opened Keep's Bank. In 1854, he was worth $60,000. He then came to New York. By 1859, he was ready to enter the pursuit of wealth. He profited largely in railroad stocks. His great achievement was in Chicago and Northwestern. A "pool" cornered the stock and Keep's share was $1,500,000. He died in 1869, leaving four and one half million dollars to his family.

Kellogg, Will K.
1860-1951

The Kellogg family gave Charles Post his inspiration. They eventually became rivals. Will K. Kellogg, the brother of the doctor who treated Post was upset because Dr. Kellogg refused to allow aggressive advertising to expand the business.

Will had to advertise in health magazines. Finally, Will broke away from his brother. He then began to build a business that became one of the leaders in the cereal industry.

By the time Kellogg died in 1951, he had built a highly successful company and a personal fortune of about $50 million.

Kennedy, Joseph Patrick
1888-1969

Joseph Patrick Kennedy amassed a fortune of close to $500 million by 1960, the year that his son John Fitzgerald Kennedy was elected President of the United States.

Joseph Kennedy was the son of a politician. He went to Harvard, and then got a job as a state bank examiner, where he learned the fundamentals of finance. In 1914, he married the daughter of Boston's Mayor, John F. "Honey Fitz" Fitzgerald.

World War I was imminent when Kennedy was hired by Charles H. Schwab to manage Bethlehem Steel's shipyard at Quincy, Massachusetts. After the war Galen stone hired Kennedy to manage the Boston office of Hayden, Stone & Co. at half the salary of Bethlehem Steel's $10,000. He sensed that he was moving into a field with greater potential.

Motion picture deals netted Kennedy millions. In one deal, he sold out all of his stock for $5 million. In 1928, he started selling off his shares. "He had a marvelous sense of timing." As the repeal of prohibition approached, he secured the American Agency for several liquor favorites. When he sold out in 1946 he got $8 million for a $100,000 investment.

In 1934, Joseph Kennedy was named Chairman of the Securities and Exchange Commission. He left after one and a half years. He was appointed to the Court of St. James in London. He urged an accommodation with the Nazis. He wanted to avoid the war.

In December, 1941 he returned to the U.S. and made millions in New York real estate. His biggest deal was for Chicago's Merchandise Mart, the world's largest building. In his waning years, he had a stroke. Kennedy moved his fortune into tax-exempt securities and an oil venture that enjoyed depletion allowances. It formed the base to back three of his sons in their successful rise to the U.S. Senate and the Presidency.

Kerkorian, Kirk
1917-

Kirk Kerkorian was born in California to American immigrant parents in 1917. He dropped out of school in the 8th grade. He became a skilled boxer in 1939. He worked with Ted O'Flaherty installing wall furnaces that heated water.

Kerkorian learned to fly. He then flew planes to Europe. He made $1,000 a flight. After the war, he bought a Cessna for $5,000. In 1947, he bought Trans International Airlines. He sold it for $104 million to Trans America Corporation.

Kirk is CEO of the Tracinda Corporation. In 1962, Kerkorian bought 80 acres of the Las Vegas Strip from the Flamingo for $960,000. This led to the building of Caesar's Palace, which rented the land from Kerkorian. He then sold the land for $9 million.

In 1967, he bought 82 acres in Las Vegas for $5 million and built The International Hotel. He also bought the Flamingo Hotel. He sold both hotels to the Hilton Hotel Corporation.

After he bought the MGM Movie Studio in 1969, he opened the MGM Grand Hotel and Casino. It burned down in a fire that was the worst disaster in Las Vegas. In 1986, Kerkorian sold the MGM Grand Hotel to Bally Mfg. for $594 million

Kerkorian's net worth was estimated at $16 billion by Forbes. He was married three times. He divides his time between Beverly Hills and Las Vegas. He is now 96 years old.

Kettering, Charles F.
1876-1958

Charles Kettering believed in research. It was the essence of his life. He devised an efficient electrical ignition system for automobiles. He founded the Dayton Engineering Laboratories Company (Delco). In 1912, he developed the first self-starter. It eliminated the hand crank. His company invented reliable headlights.

When United Motors offered to buy Delco for $9 million, Kettering sold, receiving stock as well as cash. United Motors became General Motors. In 1945, with G.M. President Alfred P. Sloan, Kettering set up the Sloan-Kettering Institute for Cancer Research in New York with a $4 million donation.

Charles Kettering did not have an interest in accumulating wealth. However, when he died at the age of eighty-two, he was worth more than $100 million and was among the fifty richest people in the United State

Keynes, John Maynard
1883-1946

John Maynard Keynes believed that government should "prime the pump" of the nation's economy to relieve unemployment. He became the guiding philosopher of the Roosevelt administration which led to the New Deal.

Keynes watched the worldwide depression and abandoned the orthodox view that low interest rates would attract business to put money into expansion. Keynes is well-known for the expression, "In the long run we are all dead."

In sum, the Keynesian view was that government could not keep its hands off business. In 1944, Keynes played a major role at the Bretton Woods Monetary and Financial Conference. He wanted to retire gold from it monetary use in exchange for a reserve money whose name he suggested should be "Bancors."

Kluge, John Werner
1914-2010

John Kluge built his fortune through a series of financial bets against the advice of his advisors. He invested in television in the 1950s. He bought FM radio stations and was the first to see the future of cellular phones.

He built Metromedia into the largest independent operator of radio and television stations. He bought 35,000 billboards, The Ice Capades, and the Harlem Globetrotters. He was married three times, and he converted to Catholicism.

In 1984, Kluge took Metromedia private and sold all his holdings. He ended up with $2.5 billion in cash. He has given more than $100 million to Columbia University. His primary home was in Charlottesville, Virginia. He was ranked third in Forbes in 1995, with a fortune estimated at $6.7 billion.

Knight, Phil
1938-

While at Stanford Graduate School of Business in the early 1960s, Phil Knight found himself in a small business class which changed his life. Professor Frank Shellenberger, "the father of small business," assigned the class the task of creating a small business, and designing a marketing plan for it. Knight's business asked, "Can Japanese Sports Shoes do to German Sports Shoes What Japanese Cameras did to German Cameras?" The paper described a plan to produce superior athletic shoes in Japan where labor costs were lower than in Germany or the United States.

"That class was an "Aha moment," Knight recalled years later. "It was what I really wanted to do." Knight's father wanted him to be an accountant. He did become an accountant, but he flew to Japan and went to Kobe to visit the Onituka Tiger Co. They made knockoffs of more expensive shoes made by Adidas. Knight made a deal to sell Tiger's shoes in the United States. He sent samples to his old track coach, Bill Bowerman, at the Universirty of Oregon. Bowerman was an Olympic coach and he was handcrafting shoes for his runners. Bowerman wanted to be Knight's partner. They each threw in $500, shook hands, and created a company in 1964. Their first employee came up with the name "Nike" after the Greek Goddess of Victory.

Sales took off and sold $3.2 million of shoes in 1972, and the next year Knight signed his first professional athlete. Nike went public in 1980. In 1984, Michael Jordan endorsed Nike. "He was a great player, He was handsome, he was articulate, he was educated, and he was perfect."

Nike has annual revenues of some $19 billion and employs more than 36,000 employees around the world. Knight remains Chairman, in Beaverton, Oregon.

Koch Family
Fred   1900-1967
Charles G. 1935-
David H.   1940-
William   1940-
Frederick R. 1933-

The Koch family of industrialists and businessmen are most notable for the control of Koch Industries, the second largest privately owned company in the United States. The family business was started by Fred C. Koch, who developed a new cracking method for the refinement of heavy oil into gasoline. Fred's four sons litigated against each other over their interests in the business during the 1980s and 1990s.

David H. Hoch and Charles G. Koch—the two brothers still with Koch Industries—are affiliated with the Koch Family Foundations. They have funded Conservative and Libertarian Policy and Advocacy Groups in the United States. Annual revenues for Koch Industries have been "estimated to be a hundred billion dollars."

Kravis, Henry R.
1944-

Henry Kravis was born in Oklahoma. He majored in Economics at Claremont College in California and in 1968 he received an MBA from Columbia University and joined the staff of Bear Stearns with his cousin George Roberts. Jerome Kohlberg, Jr. and Kravis and Roberts bought out undervalued small companies for investment. They founded Kohlberg, Kravis, Roberts & Co. (KKR).

Typically, KKR put up ten percent of the buyout price and borrowed the rest from investors by issuing "junk bonds." Their bonds were usually underwritten by Drexel, Burnham, Lambert. In the 1970s KKR bought A.J. Industries, Lily Tulip, and Houdaille Industries. The firm bought Amstar for $465 million and sold it in 1986 for $700 million. In 1987, Jerome Kohlberg retired and Henry Kravis became the senior partner.

In 1988, KKR shook up the financial world with the purchase of RJR Nabisco for $25 billion. The tobacco and food conglomerate owned Camel, Winston and Salem cigarettes, Wheat Thins, Ritz Crackers, Oreo Cookies, Fig Newtons, Del Monte Vegetables, Planters Peanuts, and Life Savers. KKR shielded Texaco from a hostile buyout and bought the Stop and Shop Grocery Chain and Duracell Battery from Kraft Foods.

In 2007, KKR exceeded their record by buying TXU for $43 to $48.billion. It was the largest corporate buyout in history. In 2010 Henry Kravis announced a gift of $100 million for Columbia to fund two new buildings for the Business School's second campus in the Manhattanville section of New York.

Kresge, Sebastian Spering
1867-1966

Sebastian Spering Kresge founded one of the 20th century's largest retail organizations. The company was renamed the Kmart Corporation in 1977, and evolved into today's Sears Holdings Corporation, parent of Kmart and Sears.

Kresge was born in Pennsylvania. He lived on the family farm until he was 21. He graduated from the Eastman Business College in 1889. On March 20, 1897, Kresge started with James G. McCrory at a five and ten cent store in Tennessee. Then, in 1899, he founded his own company with two stores for $8,000 in downtown Detroit, Michigan.

In 1912, he incorporated the S.S.Kresge Corporation with 85 stores. The chain grew into a 930 store company. It was listed on the New York Stock Exchange in 1918. By 1924, Kresge was worth about $375 million (in 1924 dollars, around $5 billion in 2009 dollars). The company owned real estate valued at $100 million. Kresge was married and divorced at least twice by 1928. He died in 1966, nine months before his 100th birthday.

Kroc, Ray Albert
1902-1984

Ray Kroc was born in Chicago. In 1922, he got a job as a salesman for the Lily Tulip Cup Company. He spent 25 years selling paper products to the convenience food industry. In the late 1930s, Earl Prince invented a milkshake mixer capable of making five shakes at a time. Kroc left Lily to gamble on the mixer to which he obtained the marketing rights. He set up his own company. World War II slowed Kroc down, but after the war he hoped that he could sell his multi-mixer to the emerging fast food restaurants.

When Ray Kroc met the McDonald brothers, he was 52 years old. He thought that he could franchise McDonald's restaurants. He decided to make McDonald's his main business. He signed as McDonald's franchising agent. It was March 2, 1955. The new company was called, McDonald's System, Incorporated. By December, 1961, Ray Kroc was ready to take over McDonald's. He purchased all rights to the McDonald's name for $2.7 million.

When Ray Kroc took control, he faced serious competition. Burger King, Burger Chef, White Castle, and Henry's were spreading throughout the country. In 1956, there were 13 McDonald's. By the end of the decade Kroc franchised more than 100 new restaurants. By the end of the 1960s the number was up to 1,000. By 1974, the figure reached 3,000.

McDonald's bought so much property, it owned more than any other corporation in the world. Franchisees introduced Filet-o-Fish, Big Macs, and Egg McMuffin. The company went public in the 1960s. The price per share soared from $22.50 to $49 in just a few weeks after the stock offering in 1965.

Kroc divorced his first wife Ethel, and 8 years later he married Joan Smith, whom he called "The ideal partner in music and marriage." Ray was now a millionaire and he set up the Kroc foundation headed by his brother Robert. In 1974, Kroc bought the San Diego Padres Baseball Team.

Today, McDonald's is the world's largest purchaser of beef and potatoes. Restaurants are all over the world, selling more than $12 billion worth of food every year. There are now over 30,000 McDonald's restaurants worldwide.

Kroger, Bernard Henry
1860-1938

Bernard Kroger was an American businessman who created the Kroger chain of supermarkets starting in 1883. Kroger was born in Cincinnati in a family of German immigrants. The family lived above their dry-goods store. Bernard Kroger was forced to go to work at age 13 to help support his family.

Kroger began working for the Great Northern and Pacific Tea Company. He became a manager. When the owners refused to make him a partner he opened his own grocery. His Great Western Tea Company was successful. He renamed the company Kroger Grocery and Baking Company, and in 1902 it was shortened to Kroger. By the end of the 1920s Kroger had opened 5,500 stores. He introduced the low-cost grocery chain models that exist today.

Kroger created the Provident Bank in 1928. During a bank crisis in 1933 he demonstrated the soundness of the bank by displaying $15 million dollars of his savings and averting a crisis. Kroger was involved in charities including parks, zoos, and medical research.

Bernard Kroger died of a heart attack in 1938 at the age of 78.

.

Land, Edwin H.
1909-1991

Edwin H. Land was a seventeen year-old Harvard freshman when he took a leave of absence to study the effect of light polarizing filters in eliminating automobile headlight glare. He returned to Harvard in 1929. In 1937 Land organized the Polaroid Corporation. Averill Harriman and Lewis Strauss gave him $375,000 in capital and a free hand. Sales of $142,000 in 1937 grew to $1,000,000 in 1941. Work in military optics increased sales to almost $17 million in 1945.

By then Land had developed a camera that could take a picture and produce a print in 60 seconds. A decade later, Polaroid Corporation had sales of $59 million and 240 patents.

Lauder, Estee
1906-2004

Josephine Esther Mentzer was born in Corona, Queens in 1906. She was one of nine children born to a Hungarian mother and a Czechoslovakian father, Max Mentzer. Much of Estee's childhood was spent helping out in the family's hardware store. Her dream was to become an actress.

Estee became interested in her uncle's (Dr. John Schotz) business. He was a chemist who owned a company called New Way Laboratories. She developed and sold creams after high school. In her early twenties she met Joseph Lauter and they married in 1930. The name was changed to Lauder. Leonard was born in 1933. In 1939 they separated when Estee moved to Florida, but remarried. In 1942 their second son Ronald was born.

In 1948 Estee persuaded the bosses of Saks Fifth Avenue to give her counter space. The rest is legend. On April 24, 2004 Estee Lauder died at the age of 97.

Law, John
1671-1729

The Mississippi Bubble is more than just a story of one of history's outstanding cases of crowd madness. It is also the fascinating biography of John Law, an unusually brilliant man who brought banking and finance to a new level of sophistication in the early years of 18th century France, almost 300 years ago.

John Law was born in Edinburgh in 1671. Before he was 24 his parents died, and he gambled and sought the society of women. His involvement with a young married lady was the cause of a duel in which Law killed his adversary. He was condemned to death, pardoned, and then thrown into prison. He escaped and fled to the continent. He returned to Scotland when he was 50 years of age.Law thought paper was preferable to gold for the requirements of business. He gambled in Paris and won large sums of money. Louis XIV died in 1715. France was bankrupt. The Duke of Orleans, Regent of France, was king. Law appreciated his genius. In 1716 he was authorized by edict a charter for his own bank. His success was astonishing and he soon had all the specie of the country in reserve. He issued bank notes payable at a fixed amount of specie. The country's trade was helped, and confidence returned. Law's notes were selling at a 15% premium. In 1718 Law's bank was declared the Royal Bank. Law began buying on time. This was the start of margin. His company's shares zoomed to 500, 600, and 750. Law was gaining favor with the Regent and an adoring public.

Law's Indian Company floated several new stock issues and kept diluting the capitalization. The Rue Quincampoix was the street where stock was traded. The company was called "The Mississippi." Soon, the inevitable happened, panic selling, a run on the bank, the bank closed. All sales and purchases were prohibited. Law fled. He returned to England, received clemency for killing the gentleman in a duel. He realized that blind confidence must inevitably lead to blind despair. He ended his life in poverty. He lived in Venice. He was destitute, miserable, and forgotten.

Lazarus, Simon
1820-1877

Simon Lazarus was the founder of the predecessor of what was to become the F & R Lazarus & Co., an operation which grew into what is today known as Macy's Inc., a major retail holding company in the U.S.

In 1850, Lazarus, a rabbinical scholar, arrived in Columbus, Ohio, and in 1851 he opened the Lazarus store. He was assisted by his sons Fred and Ralph. The mass manufacture of uniforms for the Civil War expanded the business. It led to a full line of ready-made men's civilian clothing. Simon Lazarus was the first Rabbi of Central Ohio's Oldest Reform Synagogue, Temple Israel.

Simon died in 1877. His widow Amelia and her sons Fred and Ralph ran the business and changed the name to F & R Lazarus & Company. In 1928 the company bought the John Shillito Company Department Store in Cincinnati. In 1929, Federated Department Stores Inc. was organized in Columbus as a holding company for its subsidiaries, John Shillito, William Filene's Sons & Company, and Abraham & Straus Department Stores. The Lazarus family pioneered many firsts in retailing including lobbying Franklin D. Roosevelt to permanently set the fourth Thursday in November as Thanksgiving, thereby ensuring a longer Christmas selling season in those years in which November had five Thursdays.

Lehman, House of

When Emanuel Lehman died, control of the firm was fully in the hands of the second generation- restless, eager, and ambitious boys—Philip, Sigmund, Arthur, Meyer H., and Herbert. When it came to banking Philip was ingenious. It is Philip's wizardry, along with the strength of his will and his personality. Philip had to win. Philip Lehman led his cousins into retail stores, textile manufacturing, clothing, or cigarette making. He had profitable results very quickly.

It was Philip who insisted that the firm venture into underwriting. He often discussed it with his best friend, Henry Goldman. It was Henry Goldman and Philip Lehman who told Julius Rosenwald to sell stock to the public when he wanted to expand the business. Instead of a $5 million dollar loan, Rosenwald made $10 million.

Levitt, Arthur
1931-

Arthur Levitt was the longest serving Chairman of the United States Securities and Exchange Commission (SEC), from 1993-2001. Since May 2001, he has been a senior advisor at the Carlyle Group. He is also advisor to Goldman Sachs and a director of Bloomberg. Levitt was born in Brooklyn, New York and he married Marilyn Blauner.

Levitt grew up in Brooklyn. His father, Arthur Levitt Sr. was New York State Controller for 24 years. Arthur Levitt Jr. was Phi Beta Kappa from Williams College in 1952, and then served for two years in the Air Force. In 1963, he joined Sanford Weill's firm, and it was renamed, "Cogan, Berlind, Weill, & Levitt. Mergers caused the firm to evolve into Shearson, Loeb Rhoades. Sixteen years later Levitt became Chairman of the American Stock Exchange. Levitt then owned Roll Call, a newspaper that covered Capitol Hill. In 1993 President Clinton appointed him to head the SEC.

Levitt, William
1907-1994

William Levitt started a minor revolution in home-building techniques. He was able to cut costs and speed production by means of mass production.

Near his home base in Manhasset, Long Island, Levitt & Sons, Inc. put up more than 17,000 homes in five years, creating the new community of Levittown where there had once been potato fields. He then turned to building another Levittown in Pennsylvania, a $200 million project for the housing, shopping, and recreational needs of 70,000 people.

Lewisohn, Adolph
1849-1938

Adolph Lewisohn spoke to Thomas Edison about his invention that recorded human voices. Copper wire was the answer. In 1878, all copper imported to the United States from Europe was subject to a duty of five cents a pound, but hundreds of tons that had been sold cheaply to Europe the year before could be re-imported without payment of duty. American copper was to be shipped back in the same casks. Also, the European seller had to provide a certificate saying that re-imported metal had originated in America.

The Lewisohn boys ordered copper with no such certification. It was a gamble, and it worked. The shipments passed customs untaxed, and the Lewisohns sold the copper quickly. They bought their first mine in Butte, Montana. Adolph bought the Colusa Mine and formed a company called the Montana Copper Company.

Adolph came up with the best ideas. Railroad rates depended on the quantity of ore shipped. He shipped tons of slag along with the high-grade ore at cheaper prices. Adolph had once been embarrassed checking into hotels with tiny personal effects. He bought a large suitcase and filled it with rocks.

By the 1930s the Lewisohns were considered the copper kings. One of their mines paid $35 million in dividends alone. He made so much money that Adolph started spending. He bought the Harriman Mansion at 881 Fifth Avenue, and a castle in Westchester. Adoph Lewisohn became a playboy.

In the battle for control of the American Smelting and Refining Company, Dan Guggenheim won control and made the Guggenheim's the mining kings of the world. Adolph Lewisohn had A.S.& R shares and was content to enjoy spending and enjoying his millions.

Limbaugh, Rush Hudson
1951-

Rush Limbaugh is an American radio talk show host and political commentator. He started as a disc jockey. His talk show began in 1984 in Sacramento, California on KEBK. In 1988 Limbaugh began broadcasting from radio station WABC in New York City. He currently lives in Palm Beach, Florida, He broadcasts the Rush Limbaugh Show, the highest rated talk-radio program in the United States. His audience is 15 million. Limbaugh is among the highest paid people in the U.S. media, signing a contract in 2008 for $400 million through 2016.

Rush was born in Missouri. His father was a lawyer and a U.S. fighter pilot who served in China during World War II. Limbaugh left college after two semesters. His only interest was radio. He was not drafted during the Vietnam War because of a pilonidal cyst. He was classified as 4-F

Limbaugh took jobs at several radio stations. In 1984 he replaced Morton Downey Jr. at KEBK in Sacramento, California. His success moved Rush to WABC in New York City and a nationally syndicated show. There was personal difficulty in the 2000s. Rush acknowledged that he was going deaf. Cochlear implants helped him regain his hearing.

Ling, James Joseph
1922-2004

James Ling started in business with $3,000 from the sale of his house in 1946. Under his guidance, Ling Electric went public in 1955. After the purchase of Temco Electronics and Chance Vought Corporation the company became Ling-Temco-Vought. Sales in 1962 reached $325 million.

Ling used the redeployment system, which simply spun a company into separate entities to increase the value of the parent company. In the years that followed LTV acquired the Okonite Company in 1965 and the Great America Corporation, National Car Rental, and Braniff International Airways. Wilson & Co. was split up into Wilson Sporting Goods, Wilson Pharmaceutical & Chemical Company, and the meat packing and food operations. This created separate market values for each of the parts.

In 1970, LTV had sales of $3.8 billion but difficulties in some of the divisions resulted in net losses of $70 million.

.

Livermore, Jesse Lauriston
1877-1940

Jesse Livermore, one of Wall Street's legendary speculators, liked to be called "The Boy Wonder." The farm boy from Shrewsbury, Massachusetts made and lost four multi-million dollar fortunes. He took his own life in the hat-check room of New York's Stork Club. He was deep in debt, with no hope of making another comeback.

Livermore loved the good life. He enjoyed the trappings, the women, and the fame. He was a big spender and he courted the press. His personal life was unhappy, with several wives and a playboy's love of pretty women.

The exciting years brought him wealth, yachts, Palm Beach, and rubbing elbows with the prominent people he tried to emulate. It may not be the measure of success for everybody, but it satisfied the ambition of this dirt farmer from Massachusetts.

Loeb, Gerald M.
1899-1974

Gerald Loeb achieved a stature in Wall Street that few people in our country's history have attained. He is a legend. He has been called "The Wizard of Wall Street." For more than fifty years he wrote a column in Barron's. He published a book called, "The Battle for Investment Survival" which contained his investment ideas. Loeb believed that you should "Put all your eggs in one basket and watch that basket.' In Loeb's view, "It is not enough to know the fundamentals of successful investing, it takes an extra something, experience, judgment, and flair."

Loeb, John
1902-1996
Loeb, John Jr.
1930-

Carl M. Loeb bought a seat on the New York Stock Exchange in 1931. He later merged his firm to create the Carl M. Loeb, Rhoades & Company. His son John said that he could run an investment banking house, so he bought one. It became one of the top firms in Wall Street.

John Loeb sold the firm's major Cuban sugar holdings the day before Fidel Castro took over. John Loeb's daughter Ann married Edgar Bronfman, elder son of Samuel Bronfman, the founder and CEO of Distillers Corporation-Seagrams Ltd, the richest man in Canada. At sixty-four, John Loeb, a Governor of the New York Stock Exchange was held in awe in Wall Street. He was tall, slender, and handsome.

Loeb had personal power, and financial power as well. He had the kind of influence and presence not seen on Wall Street since the days of Jacob Schiff.

Loeb, Solomon
1828-1903

Solomon Loeb was a founding member of the Kuhn, Loeb banking house. After Jacob Schiff married Solomon Loeb's daughter, things began to change in the Loeb household. Schiff was religious and Loeb was an agnostic.

In business Loeb was cautious and Schiff was bold. About ten years after Jacob Schiff became a partner, Solomon Loeb abdicated and allowed Jacob Schiff to direct the policy of Kuhn, Loeb.

Loew, Marcus
1870-1927

Marcus Loew was a pioneer in the motion picture industry who formed Loew's Theatres and Metro-Goldwyn-Mayer (MGM).

Marcus was born into a poor family in New York City. He had little formal education and was forced to work at a very young age. He saved money and bought into a penny arcade business. He partnered with Adolph Zukor and bought a Nickelodeon. Over time he turned Loew's Theatres into the most prestigious chain of movie theatres in the United States.

Loew's large chain of theatres needed a steady stream of motion pictures. He purchased Metro Pictures, Goldwyn Pictures Corporation, and Louis B. Mayer's company. This led to the founding of Metro-Goldwyn-Mayer (MGM) in 1924. Mayer's chief of production Irving Thalberg was included in the development of the company.

Loew died three years after MGM was formed, in 1927, and never got to see the powerhouse that it was to become. He was interred in the Maimonides Cemetery in Brooklyn.

Longworth, Nicholas
1782-1863

Longworth was the largest landowner in Cincinnati. He assembled farmland and held it until it became part of the growing metropolis. His fortune was estimated at $15 million.

Longworth was born in Newark, New Jersey. He was trained as a shoemaker. In 1805, with no more than the clothes that he wore he arrived in Cincinnati. The population was only 800 people. He studied law under a judge and became a lawyer in six months. One case that he won resulted in the acquisition of 33 acres of land. That was how he got into real estate. He continued his law practice and constantly added to his land holdings. He founded a vineyard and produced 500,000 bottles of wine per year.

When he died in 1863, at 81, he left his fortune to his son and three daughters.

Lord & Taylor

Samuel Lord was born in Yorkshire, England in 1803, the youngest of nine children. At 6 years of age he was orphaned and at an early age he worked at James Taylor's foundry. When he was twenty-one, he married the proprietor's daughter, and a few months later set out for the new world to seek his fortune. He opened a small retail store in New York on the Bowery. He borrowed a thousand dollars from his wife's uncle, John Taylor. He enlarged his store and took his wife's cousin, George Washington Taylor into partnership.

Mr. Taylor retired to Manchester, England in 1852. Samuel Lord built an elegant marble structure at Grand Street and Broadway. Around 1860 Lord took his son and a clerk, John S. Lyle into partnership and retired to England at Ashton-on-Mersey in Cheshire.

As the shopping district moved north, Lord & Taylor took steps to move further uptown. Several moves later, with Edward P. Hatch as manager, Lord & Taylor established the present store on Thirty-Ninth Street corner of Fifth Avenue in 1914. Presidents Samuel Reyburn and Walter Hoving followed, and business flourished for one of the most beautiful retail establishments in the world.

Branch stores were built in Manhasset, Long Island, Scarsdale, New York, Millburn, New Jersey, West Hartford, Connecticut, Bala Cynwyd, Pennsylvania, Garden City, Long Island, and Washington, D.C.

Lorillard, Pierre
1742-1776

The French-born Pierre Lorillard set up the first tobacco factory in America in New York City in 1760. He prospered by making pipe and snuff tobacco with a special recipe. Pierre was killed by Hessian mercenaries during the revolution.

Pierre's sons moved the factory north of New York City in 1792. In the 1830s the company was distributed nationally. Pierre IV was born in 1833. He owned 7,000 acres in Orange County New York. It became a club called Tuxedo Park.

After becoming part of the giant American Tobacco Company, the Supreme Court broke the trust into American Tobacco, Liggett & Myers, and P. Lorillard. Today, the company is part of the Loew's Corporation. Some of the brands have been Old Gold, Murad, Between the Acts, and Kent.

Love, James Spencer
1896-1965

In 1923, J. Spencer Love built a plant for the production of textiles in Burlington, North Carolina. He turned to a new and untried fiber—Rayon. The new mill began weaving a blend of Rayon and Cotton. The first new product was a bedspread. The foundation for the future growth of Burlington Industries was formed. By 1937 Burlington was the world's largest weaver of rayon fabric with thirty-two plants and sales volume of $27 million. By 1962 Burlington had become a significant force in the nation's economy. Sales that year reached $1.3 billion. After Spencer Love's death in 1965 the new management aggressively diversified the manufacture of fabrics for apparel, home, and industry.

The company which Love founded in 1923 began its fiftieth year (1973) with 135 plants in the United States, 84,000 employees, and sales in 1972 of $1.8 billion.

Ludwig, Daniel K.
1897-1992

Daniel Ludwig bought his first boat at the age of eight. It was a sunken wreck—for $25. He built a large and powerful fleet of supertankers and became a dominant force in U.S. shipping.

He diversified his holdings into other businesses. He lost a large part of his wealth in a scheme to harvest wood pulp from the Amazon jungle. His fortune remained at over $1 billion.

Mackey, John
1953-

It started in Austin, Texas. John Mackey and his girl friend began selling bulk foods and produce and slept on a futon in an office above the store. This was the humble beginning of Whole Foods Market.

Today, after years of difficult times, Whole Foods Market has more than 300 supermarkets in North America and the United Kingdom. It employs 60,000 people and its revenue will top $10 billion in 2011.

John Mackey admitted to "socialist leanings" in his early years, but today he is an evangelist for Capitalism, and an admirer of Milton Friedman, Ayn Rand, and Ronald Reagan.

MacArthur, John Donald
1897-1978

John D. MacArthur was an American businessman who made his fortune in the insurance business. In 1935 he acquired the Bankers Life and Casualty Company for $2,500. He built his insurance empire through acquisitions of many small insurance corporations. In the 1950s MacArthur hired broadcaster Paul Harvey to be the radio spokesman for the company.

Macarthur increased his vast fortune by investing in Florida real estate. In 1954 he bought 2,500 acres of land in Palm Beach County for $5.5 million. MacArthur was born in Pittsburgh, Pennsylvania. He and his many brothers and sisters grew up in poverty, the children of a Baptist preacher. MacArthur's sister-in-law was the actress Helen Hayes.

Macarthur had two children with his first wife. In 1928 he married Catherine T. MacArthur who managed his companies and his charitable foundation. Bankers Life today is a leader in Long Term Care Insurance in the U.S. The company is publicly held and is capitalized at about $6 billion. It is a subsidiary of the Conseco Insurance Companies.

Macy, Rowland Hussey
1822-1877

Rowland H. Macy was born on Nantucket Island, Massachusetts. He had several dry-goods businesses and he and his brother went out west during the gold rush in 1849. His general store, Macy & Company broke up quickly and was sold at a small profit.

Macy's son was a ne'er-do-well and it led to other people assuming the management of the company. Macy died in 1877 at the age of fifty-four. His estate was $300,000. The concession of the china and glass departments to the Straus brothers had a great influence on the future of Macy's.

Eventually, Isidor and Nathan Straus bought complete control of Macy's in 1896 for $1,200,000. In 1901 Isidor's two sons Jesse and Percy, who were active in the store, selected a location on the west side of Herald Square at Thirty-Fourth Street. The business was incorporated as R.H. Macy & Co. in 1919, with all the stock held by the Straus family until the first issue to the public in 1922. Macy's additions to the store in 1928 and 1931 gave Macy's its title of the largest department store in the world.

Expansion continued and Macy's comprised 32 units all over the country. The sales figure for all the stores in the chain was about $465,000,000 per annum. The staff was 11,000 and there were 168 selling departments. If you fly over the Manhattan store, the roof has the following slogan, "It's smart to be thrifty. That's Macy's."

Magee, John
1901-1987

John Magee is the father of technical analysis. He and Bob Edwards authored the definitive textbook on technical analysis, "Technical Analysis of Stock Trends."

Magee was fanatical about keeping his mind free of fundamental contamination. He didn't care what the company made, what industry it was in, or what products it produced. He locked himself in his office and did not care to hear the radio announcing the news.

Technical analysis is not a science. Charting is open to interpretation. The benefit of charts is that they are easy to maintain. All you need is a pencil, paper, and the daily stock market quotes.

Magee had a son from his first marriage and another son and two daughters from a second marriage. He was born in Malden, Massachusetts in 1901 and graduated from MIT in 1923. Richard W. Schabacker was Bob Edwards' brother-in-law. He was the first one to apply the chart method to individual stocks.

John Magee started his own firm, "Stock Trend Services," and in Springfield, Massachusetts he taught an adult-education program for a decade. This led to his book which has sold millions of copies. Magee died in 1987 at 86. He is unquestionably considered the dean of technical analysis and he gave birth to the process of predicting the direction of stock prices based on charts.

Marcus, Bernie
1929-

It was the best thing that happened in their lives. "Ming the Merciless" (Sandy Sigoloff) was the boss from hell. He was the CEO of Handy-Dan's Home Improvement Central. He loved to fire people. Both Bernie Marcus and Arthur Blank were given the ax. They were devastated. Did they quit? Did they give up? No!

Bernie was 48 and Arthur was 34. They took everything they learned and created one of the most successful retail concepts in history. They developed the (DIY) do-it-yourself business. Here's what they did. They built warehouse stores, 75,000 square feet (twice the size of Handy Dan's). They bought direct from the manufacturers, eliminated the middleman, and put highly trained people on the selling floor. From the first store in 1979 it took two decades for Bernie Marcus and Arthur Blank to build a chain of 1,200 outlets in North and South America, which had annual sales of $46 billion dollars. The name of their stores is Home Depot.

They are still close friends, and play golf with Ken Langone, who was an early investor with $2 million dollars of seed capital.

McCormick, Cyrus
1809-1884

Cyrus McCormick chose Chicago to set up his factory. It was the hub of the new Northwest growing area. Chicago's former mayor, William Ogden put up $25,000 for a half interest in a partnership. They manufactured 500 horse-drawn mechanical reapers for the 1848 harvest. Two years later McCormick bought out Ogden for $50,000.

McCormick was the first great industrialist of the Chicago area. In 1848 Chicago was a swamp---in 1855, engineers dredged the Chicago River and began to build a great city.

McCullough, J.F.
1871-1963
The Kings of Dairy Queen

J.F. McCullough started selling ice cream in 1927. He was 56 years old. He bought a cheese factory and converted it to an ice cream plant. He noticed that soft ice cream tasted better than the frozen product.

He needed a machine that could make soft ice cream at the store. He noticed a frozen custard stand in Chicago. It was just what he was looking for. "Grandpa McCullough" tracked down the manufacturer, Harry M. Oltz. They worked out a contract. McCullough's first employee, Herb Klavohn tinkered with Oltz's invention and grandpa found that 5 to 6 percent butterfat and 18 degrees Fahrenheit was the ideal temperature for soft serve ice cream.

Joliet, Illinois had the first "Dairy Queen." On June 22, 1940 the second store opened in Moline, Illinois. The success was immediate. Harry Axene saw the long lines at the Dairy Queen store. He wanted in. The 72-year-old McCullough was ready to retire. Axene was offered half ownership of his company and the right to operate Dairy Queens in Iowa and Illinois for $12,000.

Axene liked the franchise strategy. 26 investors met in Moline, Illinois. Axene offered a territory and exclusive right to operate Dairy Queens. They would pay 19 to 34 cents a gallon. A one -time payment was as much as $100,000 for a large territory. Before the meeting there were 8 Dairy Queens. Two years later, there were 100 stores. In 1948 there were 400 stores, and 1,400 two years later. Within a decade, Dairy Queen had grown into the largest and most widespread food-service franchise system in the world. In 1948, Axene had sold all of his Dairy Queen territories. He had no reason to stay with the company, and left a year later.

The number of stores reached 3,000 by 1960. International Dairy Queen enjoyed dramatic growth through the 1970s and 1980s. By 1980, the company's 4,833 stores passed the $1 billion mark in sales.

In 1998 the Berkshire Hathaway Corporation in Omaha led by Warren Buffett assumed control of IDQ which had 5,800 Dairy Queen srores serving customers in the United States and Canada.

McCrory, John G.

John McCrory was the founder of the McCrory Five and Ten Cent Store chain. He was born in Pennsylvania. He moved to Johnstown, Pennsylvania when he was 18 and began working in retail stores. At age 22 he opened the first store in Scottsdale, Pennsylvania. It would become a chain of hundreds of McCrory stores. It was the second of the great five and dime chain stores founded at the end of the nineteenth century, following F.W. Woolworth (1879) and preceded those of S.S.Kresge (1899). The latter chain was renamed Kmart.

McCrory is interred in the family mausoleum whose entrance is inscribed "McRorey," the original spelling of the family name.

McDonald, Maurice and McDonald, Richard
1902-1971 and 1909-1998

The McDonald brothers grew up in Bedford, New
Hampshire. When the shoe factory where their father was
foreman closed down during the depression, the boys
headed west to California.

In 1937 they opened a hot dog stand and gradually
switched to hamburgers. In 1940, they built a larger store
near San Bernardino, California. Drive-ins were popular,
and the McDonald's parking lot could accommodate 125
cars. The restaurant made $50,000 a year. However, the
McDonald brothers grew bored with the business. Teen
agers dominated their trade and it became a hangout which
was avoided by families. Carhops kept quitting after a few
weeks, silverware was disappearing, and competition was
beginning to worry them.

The McDonalds revamped their business. They
reduced the menu to only nine items, and lowered the price
of burgers to fifteen cents from thirty cents. Families were
thrilled that they could buy a meal at a reasonable price,
with no waiting.

In 1951, sales were $277,400, up 40 percent from
carhop days. Over the next two years the McDonalds sold
15 franchises and their profits rose to more than $100,000
a year. One of their suppliers, Ray Kroc, offered to
franchise the McDonald's system in 1954. In 1961, Kroc
bought all the rights to use and license the McDonald's
name. The brothers dropped out of the restaurant scene,
leaving their name behind.

Mellon, Andrew W. and Mellon, Richard
1855-1937 and 1858-1933

Andrew and Richard Mellon were two brothers who worked together and acted as one in the management of the Mellon bank. Their father, Judge Thomas Mellon immigrated to Pittsburgh in 1818, when he was five. After a career on the bench, he established a bank, T. Mellon & Sons. He had eight children. Andrew and Richard followed Thomas at the bank in Pittsburgh.

The Mellon brothers at the bank built the Aluminum Corporation of America, the Carborundum Abrasives Company, the Koppers Coke Company and many other enterprises. They bought a controlling interest in a Texas oil strike that became Gulf Oil. At age sixty-five the retiring Andrew Mellon was appointed Secretary of the Treasury by President Warren G. Harding in 1921. He was later appointed Ambassador to Great Britain. Andrew had to resign from the boards of fifty-one corporations to avoid a conflict of interest.

Andrew Mellon was the last Secretary of the Treasury to reduce the National Debt. The Mellon's gave a great deal of money to charity. By the time Andrew died he only had $37 million in his estate. Richard's son, Richard King Mellon carried on the family's business. Andrew's son Paul had no interest in the family's business. He gave away $250 million in paintings. In 1995, when Paul was 88 years old, his fortune was estimated at $1 billion. Forbes estimated the Mellon fortune in 1995 to be $5.4 billion.

.

Monaghan, Tom
1937-

Tom Monaghan struggled through a difficult childhood. His father died when he was four years old. He grew up in foster homes and he grew distant from his mother. In the ninth grade he decided to become a priest. He was accepted into a seminary in Grand Rapids, Michigan. He couldn't follow the rules and was expelled after a few months. His Aunt Peg gained custody of him. He finished high school with mediocre grades.

He joined the Marines to make enough money to pay for college. He lost all his money on an investment with a stranger who picked him up on a pass to Las Vegas. He returned to Ann Arbor and moved in with his brother Jim. He worked at a store where they sold pizza and submarine sandwiches. He bought a store for $9,500 in Ypsilanti, Michigan with his brother Jim. Eight months later Jim pulled out. Tom Monaghan weathered many storms and began expanding. By 1978 he had 200 stores. By 1980 he had 440, and he reached 1,000 in 1983.

In 1983 Monaghan bought the Detroit Tigers baseball team. He survived a lawsuit by Amstar which wanted him to change his name. Domino Sugar was in business long before Domino's Pizza. Domino's success is based on speedy delivery of hot pizza. 30 minute delivery is Domino's promise. Domino's has grown to 6,000 stores in the year 2000, and delivers more than 6 million pizzas a week. In September, 1998 Tom Monaghan retired. Bain Capital, Inc. acquired a 93 percent stake in Domino's from the Monaghan family.

Morgan, John Pierpont
1837-1913

J.P. Morgan is one of the greatest figures in American financial history. Morgan's formation of United States Steel was a landmark achievement at the start of the twentieth century (1901). The great Morgan was forced to extend himself to achieve his goal. A canny Scot, Andrew Carnegie, the best steel man in America was ready to retire, but he rallied his enormous resources to simulate a great expansion just as Morgan was about to buy him out. In the end it cost Morgan $492 million. Morgan got his money back, and then some, when he capitalized United States Steel at $1,402 million.

The American reading public also shared in Carnegie's triumph since the $350 million he bequeathed to the country was used to build thousands of libraries. Carnegie gave away almost all of his fortune because he truly believed, "He who dies rich dies disgraced."

The House of Morgan soared into prominence after Jay Cooke's failure in 1873. The railroads had made a fortune for Gould and Vanderbilt, but overexpansion and speculation had pumped $4 billion into railroad capitalizations. In 1884 the gigantic structure of inflated railroads crashed. Morgan moved in to reorganize several railroad systems into solvency. including Baltimore & Ohio, Chesapeake & Ohio, Philadelphia & Reading, Pennsylvania Railroad, and the Southern Railway System. J.P. Morgan was a giant figure in railroads and banking. He had largely reorganized the entire railroad system of America. At the turn of the century he stood alone, healthy, vigorous, and prominent in his field. All of his partners had died.

J.P. Morgan was a bull on America. His character had formed by 1884—stubborn courage, tremendous arrogance, and cynicism. Morgan was a man of heroic remedies, a domineering man of destiny. Chauncey Depew and Vanderbilt were locked in aboard the Corsair, Morgan's yacht. Morgan, 6 feet, 200 pounds, sprawled in a chair with his ever present black cigar, refereeing an agreement which had to be made before the yacht cruise was ended. The hostages to Morgan's brusque dominance smoked the peace pipe and Morgan collected $1-3 million dollars in commissions.

Morgan was imperiously proud, intensely undemocratic, throwing food and clothing at his servants. He lived openly with one woman and appeared in public with another. In 1894 the Secretary of the Treasury was compelled to go to Morgan for a $50,000,000 loan to purchase foreign gold. Morgan saved the country at usurious rates. In 1895, with gold drained away by hoarders, Grover Cleveland was forced to come to Morgan. Cleveland refused to pay the "pound of flesh" as Morgan played solitaire in his Washington hotel and the gold supply of the country sank to a one day supply. President Cleveland submitted to the master of Wall Street. J.P.Morgan and John D. Rockefeller hated each other. They were constantly vying for predominance in rank, but both had a domain that demanded the awe of kings.

Morgan, Junius Spencer
1813-1890

Junius Spencer Morgan , the father of J.P. Morgan left Boston for London in 1854 when John Pierpont Morgan was only a teenager. J.S. Morgan sent his son to Goettingen for several years before sending him to New York as a clerk for the firm's American representative. That was during the Panic of 1857. Morgan joined one of Philadelphia's oldest banking houses to form Drexel, Morgan and Company, making that old-line firm even stronger with Morgan's New York presence under its umbrella.

Morse, Samuel F.B.
1791-1872

Samuel Morse was the inventor of an electrical method of sending coded letters over the wire. It is called The Morse Code. Congress awarded Morse $30,000 dollars to build a demonstration line. His first message was "What hath God wrought!"

With the help of Ezra Cornell telegraph lines were built connecting many of the major cities (New York, Boston, Cleveland, Chicago, Detroit, and Buffalo).

The telegraph increased the impact and importance of newspapers which grew from 150 in 1800 to 2,800 in 1850.

Murchison, Clinton Williams
1923-1987

Clint Murchison made money in cattle, but more in oil. He switched early in his life, and with his lifelong friend Sid Richardson he began trading oil leases. He wildcatted his way to an income of $30,000 a month. In the late 1920s he sold his interests for $5 million and retired. He went back to investing in companies. "what else is a fellow to do—I can't play the piano."

In the 1930s he built the Southern Union Gas Company to sell the natural gas other oil men thought was not marketable. If you had bought 10,000 shares of the utility for $1 a share in 1942 you would have made a profit of $2.8 million. By 1943 Murchison was a giant conglomerate. He owned cattle ranches, chemical companies, Dallas's only taxicab service, a life insurance company, the Martha Washington Candy Makers, a fishing tackle plant, and a 75,000 acre ranch in Mexico.

In addition, he bought control of the American Mail Line, the Henry Holt Publishing Company, a chain of theaters, a Mexican silverware factory, The Diebold Office Equipment Firm, Field & Stream Magazine, public utilities, banks, and Royal Gorge Bridge and its amusement facilities.

Murchison's philosophy was, "money is like manure. If you spread it around, it does a lot of good, but if you pile it up in one place, it stinks like hell." When Clint Murchison died, he owned more than 100 enterprises worth more than $300 million.

Neiman-Marcus
A.L. Neiman

1875-1970

Herbert Marcus
1878-1950

Herbert Marcus and his sister Carrie and her husband A.L. Neiman opened a high-fashion store in Dallas in the early years of the 20th century. Herbert and Carrie were born in Louisville, Kentucky. Herbert arrived in Hillsboro, Texas in 1893. He worked in his brother's store and then worked his way to Dallas where he was a buyer for Sanger Brothers. Carrie was an assistant buyer at A. Harris in 1905, when she met her husband A.L. (Al) Neiman.

Herbert's son Stanley was born and because he couldn't get a raise, Herbert resigned and went to Atlanta, Georgia with his partner, A.L. Neiman. After two years, they had an opportunity to sell out. They were offered $25,000 in cash or Coca Cola stock. Wow! They could have been millionaires. They chose the cash and opened a new kind of store in Dallas. From the start, theirs was to be a store selling the finest in fashion.

Their store opened on September 10, 1907. By the end of four weeks they had sold almost all of their stock. Several fires trace the history of Neiman-Marcus. All the merchandise was disposed of by Filene's. To keep pace with the growth of Dallas, many expansions were undertaken between 1927 and World War II. In the post-war era, $7,500,000 in 1951 doubled the store's capacity.

Through the years Herbert Marcus and his sister Carrie guided the business to its high standing in the fashion world. A.L. Neiman sold his Neiman-Marcus interests to Herbert Marcus in 1928 when he parted from Carrie and went to Paris to run his own business. Herbert Marcus's four sons (Stanley, Edward, Herbert Jr., and Lawrence) entered the business. Herbert Sr. lost his sight in 1946 and died at the age of 75 in 1950. In 1953, Mrs. Carrie Neiman died at the age of 70. The Neiman-Marcus name has always retained the reputation that the founders envisioned. It has lasted even until today.

Nelson, Samuel A.

As one of the early admirers of Charles Dow, S.A. Nelson tried to persuade him to write a book incorporating his ideas and writings. For some reason, Dow refused and never did put his thoughts together into a comprehensive framework.

Nelson did the next best thing, however, and was able to get permission to reprint several of Dow's editorials from the Wall Street Journal. These essays form the basis of what Nelson termed, "The Dow Theory." Although the editorials are advice for speculators, they are actually the basis of modern technical analysis.

Newhouse, Samuel I.
1895-1979

Starting with $2 a week "Sammy" Newhouse was told to take care of the Bayonne News by his boss Hyman Lazarus. Newhouse was the oldest of eight children of poor immigrants. He quit school at thirteen to help support the family. Newhouse took that failing paper and had it running in the black. That was the start of a career of turning around failing newspapers for S.I. Newhouse. By the time of his death in 1979, he controlled an empire of 31 newspapers, 7 magazines, 6 television stations, 5 radio stations, and 20 cable systems. Revenues were $750 million.

His company was worth over $1 billion and was the most valuable private company in the nation. He had complete control of his holdings and had no debt. S.I. Newhouse left the company to his two sons, Donald and S.I. Jr. By 1995 the Newhouse brothers were listed as sharing an $8.4 billion dollar fortune.

Ohrbach, Nathan M.
1885-1972

Nathan Ohrbach was born in Vienna in 1885. Two years later he was in Brooklyn. At 14 he worked in a clothing store for $3.50 a week. He became a buyer for several stores. In 1911 he opened a specialty shop, Bon Marche on Fulton Street in Brooklyn. Ohrbach soon acquired a location on 14th Street in Manhattan (between Fifth Avenue and University Place).

Nathan Ohrbach and Max Wiesen, a dress manufacturer took over a derelict 27 foot frontage space which was a penny arcade and Nickelodeon owned by film pioneer Adolph Zukor. A considerable sum was spent converting the space to a women's wear store. The grand opening on October 4, 1923 drew a large crowd. Success was immediate. Sales in 1924 were over $1,500,000. Expansion was inevitable. Adjoining premises were acquired. Five years later, in 1928, Wiesen sold his interest for ten times the $62,000 he invested.

Ohrbach and his son Jerome expanded nationwide and his 34th Street store was leased from James McCreery. The eleven-story store was remodeled at a cost of $2 million. The first day's business was made in August, 1954. 100,000 persons spent $500,000 to kick off Ohrbach's new store.

Olin, John Merrill
1892-1982

John Olin was born in Alton, Illinois. He graduated from Cornell University with a B.S. Degree in Chemistry. He was married twice.

Olin started his career with his father at Western Cartridge Company, the predecessor of Olin Industries. In 1935 Western Cartridge acquired Winchester Repeating Arms Company. John Olin became President of Olin Industries and became Chairman of the Olin Mathieson Chemical Corporation when Olin merged with Mathieson. In 1963 he became honorary Chairman of the Board.

Olin had 24 patents in the field of arms and ammunition. He bred and raced thoroughbred race horses and won the Kentucky Derby with the colt Cannonade. John Merrill Olin died in 1982 at the age of 89, in his home in East Hampton, New York.

Otis, Elisha Graves
1811-1861

Elisha Graves Otis invented the elevator in 1852. In 1853 he opened the first plant to manufacture elevators. It was the start of a company and an industry.

When Elisha Otis died of Diphtheria during the 1861 epidemic, his sons Charles and Norton continued the business. In 1889 Otis introduced the electric elevator. Today, computer systems with solid state circuitry control whole groups of elevators for split-second response to passenger calls.

Packard, David
1912-1996

David Packard and Bill Hewlett started their business in a garage. When Packard died in 1996 at the age of eighty-three, the company had more than 100,000 employees and revenues of $31 billion.

Packard majored in electrical engineering at Stanford University. He was tall and athletic. He was a track star and earned letters in football and basketball. He met Hewlett at Stanford.

With $538, Packard and Hewlett started the company in a rented garage. By 1995 Forbes estimated Packard's fortune at $3.7 billion. Hewlett had $2.7 billion. The two partners gave $300 million to Stanford in gifts to honor their mentor professor Terman.

Packard donated more than $1 billion during his lifetime. He gave $4.5 billion of his stock to his family foundation. It is one of the richest in the nation—worth more than $7 billion.

Page, Larry and Brin, Sergey
1973-   1973-

Larry Page and Sergey Brin met at Stanford. They moved into a garage and the world changed. It was 1995. Page was twenty-two and Brin was twenty-one. They created one of the most disruptive and innovative companies in the world. Page was born into a house that had computers all over the place. Brin was born in Odessa and when the family emigrated to the United States, Sergey was six years old. He graduated with honors from the University of Maryland. He then moved to California as his interest in computer service grew.

Page and Brin named the company Google after the term "googol," referring to 1 with a hundred zeros after it. They attracted Eric Schmidt, a co-founder of Sun Microsystems, who wrote a $100,000 check. Schmidt helped to bring Google public in 2004 and helped to lead its massive growth. In Page's last year as CEO, Google's revenues exceeded $29 billion and net profits were $8.5 billion. There were more than 28,000 employees. Page took back the CEO's job and Brin focuses on product development. Google's stock price is now 1,000.

Paley, William S.
1901-1990

Starting as a cigar maker in Philadelphia, William S. Paley built the Columbia Broadcasting System into one of the leading radio and television businesses. Paley left the cigar business to become President of United Independent Broadcasters, renamed the Columbia Broadcasting System.

At twenty-eight Paley owned 16 stations that stretched from Philadelphia to Council bluffs, Iowa. By 1935 CBS had 97 stations and claimed to be the world's largest network. In 1937 it grossed $34.2 million. Paley used stars such as Kate Smith, Bing Crosby, and Morton Downey to draw audiences from NBC.

Paley astutely hired Edward R. Murrow and Frank Stanton to concentrate on news and mass popularity. In the new television medium, CBS's profits went from $25 million to $49 million from 1959 to 1964. Broadcasting came to represent only one of four divisions of CBS, which owned record and book clubs, two publishing houses, toy and musical instrument manufacturing firms, and even the New York Yankees. In 1969 CBS grossed $1 billion dollars.

Peabody, George
1795-1869

George Peabody was born in the town that now bears his name. The revolution was only a decade past. Peabody became a financial bridge between England and America. He was respected for his business acumen and generous philanthropy on both sides of the Atlantic.

Peabody was born in extreme poverty and left school at age eleven. By 1814 he was manager of a wholesale dry-goods house in Baltimore. He soon became a partner. Peabody settled in London to build a financial firm, George Peabody & Company. Although he lived in London he was a strong supporter of American securities and businesses. He competed with the Rothschilds and Barings for sales of American securities. He recruited Junius Spencer Morgan as a partner in 1854, who would help found a powerful financial house in the United States, run by his son J.P. Morgan.

During the Panics of 1837 and beyond, Peabody restored confidence in the credit worthiness of America. His confidence was well-founded, and he sold his holdings at a large profit. Peabody never married. He kept a mistress in Brighton, England with whom he had a daughter. He never gave up his American citizenship although he lived in England most of his life. When he died in 1869 at the age of seventy-four, there were two funerals—one in Westminster Abbey in London, and one by the special order of President Grant. The transcontinental funeral procession was accompanied by the American ship USS Plymouth. American friends attended his funeral at Salem, Massachusetts.

Penney, John Cash
1875-1971

In 1903 John Cash Penney opened his first store in
Wyoming. By 1911 he had twenty-two stores. The chain
grew to 312 in 1921. Sales were $46 million. It took
Macy's in New York sixty-three years to reach that sales
mark. By 1950, J.C. was still active, and there were 1,600
retail outlets, almost all of them west of the Mississippi.

When he died, at the age of 96, his company was the
nation's fourth largest retailer.

Perelman, Ronald Owen
1943-

Perelman's business empire is vast and diversified. He
has added more than forty businesses. They are held in
MacAndrews & Forbes Holding. Perelman fully controls
the company at the center of his $5 billion empire.
Perelman was raised as a dealmaker. His father Raymond,
a Lithuanian immigrant, built Belmont Industries in
Philadelphia. His businesses earned $350 million in 1987.
At the age of 75 Raymond Perelman took over Champion
Parts, Inc. after ousting the CEO.

Ron Perelman grew up going to board meetings and
reading annual reports. After graduating from the Wharton
School, he went to work for his father. After a decade,
Perelman established his own firm in New York City.

Ron bought Technicolor for $100 million and sold it for $625 million. He grew Coleman from $575 million in 1993 to $950 million in 1995. He built Revlon into the world's largest cosmetics business. He bid for Gillette and received $39 million in greenmail when his bid failed. He buys underdogs and runs them more efficiently.

Perelman has been married three times. He plans to leave his assets to his heir apparent, his oldest son Steve. " I plan to leave my assets to my children, so they should be interested in running them."

Pew, Joseph Newton
1848-1912

Joseph Newton Pew was the founder of the Sun Oil Company (Sunoco), and a prominent philanthropist. He was born in Pennsylvania. He worked on the family's farm as a child. After school he was a teacher and a real estate broker. Eventually he invested in Pennsylvania oil fields. With several partners, he began piping natural gas. He founded several petroleum-related companies, and in 1880 he incorporated the Sun Oil Company.

After Pew's death in 1912, his sons J. Howard Pew and Joseph H. Pew Jr. took over management of the company, and with their sisters founded the Pew Charitable Trusts.

Phipps, Henry
1839-1930

Henry Phipps was a shrewd partner of the Carnegie brothers-Andrew and Thomas. Phipps acquired a majority interest in an iron foundry which Kloman & Company built.

Henry Phipps was a perfect "inside man," parsimonious and crafty in the pursuit of credit for their enterprises. It was said of him that he knew how to keep a check in the air as long as any man.

Post, Charles W.
1854-1914

Charles W. Post, suffering from a nervous breakdown, went to a sanitarium in Battle Creek, Michigan. There he became interested in health foods. He bought a small farm, and with a helper developed a cereal called Postum, which he offered to the public in 1895.

In 1897 he brought out the first ready-to-eat cereal product called Grape-Nuts, because of its nutty flavor. Post Toasties was developed in 1904.

Pritzker Family

The Pritzker family is one of the wealthiest families in the United States. The family owns the Hyatt Hotel Chain, the Marmon Group, a conglomerate of manufacturing and industrial service companies. Other holdings have included the Superior Bank of Chicago, the Trans-Union Credit Bureau, the tobacco company Conwood, and the Royal Caribbean Cruise Line.

The patriarch was Naphtali Pritzker

Jacob Pritzker   1831-1896

Nicholas Pritzker 1871-1956   An immigrant from the Ukraine, founder of Pritzker & Pritzker law firm.

Harry Pritzker   1893-1957

Ann Pritzker   1896-1986 - Matriarch of family business enterprise.

Jay Pritzker   1922-1999 - Co-founder of Hyatt.

Thomas Pritzker   1951- Chief executive of the Pritzker organization.

Robert Pritzker 1926-2011- Founder of the Marmon Group.

Donald Pritzker 1932-1972 - Co-founder and President of Hyatt.

Jack Pritzker 1904-1979 - Real estate developer.

Nicholas J. Pritzker 1944- Chairman and CEO of Hyatt.

12 family members have a total net value of $196 billion dollars.

Pulitzer, Joseph
1847-1911

Joseph Pulitzer arrived in the United States from Bupapest, Hungary as a teenager. He couldn't speak English and he had no money. He slept on park benches. When he died in 1911 he owned the leading daily newspaper in New York and he had a fortune estimated at $30 million.

Pulitzer joined the Union Army and fought in the Civil War. After the war he found a job as a reporter for a German-language newspaper. He became a citizen in 1867. He bought a newspaper and he studied English and law. Pulitzer was admitted to the bar in 1875. He then bought the St. Louis Post-Dispatch for $2,500. In one year he doubled the circulation. By 1881 the paper was producing profits of $45,000 a year.

During a stop in New York, Jay Gould sold Pulitzer "the World" for $346,000 in installments. He built the World into one of the leading dailies in the country. Within three years the paper was earning half a million dollars a year in profits. His ill health caused him to give up active control of the World, and William Randolph Hearst forced him into the depths of "yellow journalism." By the time of his death in 1911, the World had a circulation of 300,000 daily and 600,000 Sunday. The Evening World sold 400,000 per day. He left most of his $30 million to his family. He left $100,000 to his employees. Pulitzer also left $2 million to set up a Journalism School in Columbia University. He is best known for the Pulitzer Prize in Literature and Journalism, funded by $500,000 of his gift to Columbia University.

Pullman, George M.
1831-1897

It was on a trip from New York to Chicago that George Pullman came up with the idea that sleeping conditions on railroad trains would revolutionize rail travel. He had to prove it could be done. In 1858, when he was twenty-seven, he persuaded a railroad to remodel three coaches into sleeping cars.

After a few years where Pullman had a general store in the Colorado mining fields, he organized the Pullman Palace Car Company with his partner Ben Field. It became the biggest railroad car manufacturer in the world. Commodore Vanderbilt and Carnegie backed competitors, but Pullman was the leading company in the industry.

Pullman created a whole town, Pullman, Illinois which was eventually absorbed into Chicago. A bitter strike took its toll on his fortune, but he had an estate of $175 million. He didn't trust his twin sons, and left them only $3,000 a year in his will. His wife was successful in getting the principle, and was prominent in society and philanthropy until her death in 1921.

Raskob, John Jakob
1879-1950

John Jakob Raskob was a financial executive and businessman for DuPont and General Motors. He built the Empire State Building.

Raskob was born in Lockport, New York. His father had a successful cigar business. The Raskob family came from Germany. Raskob delivered newspapers and was active in the Catholic community. He dropped out of school to support his family after his father died in 1898.

He was hired by Pierre S. DuPont as a personal secretary. He worked his way up to Vice President for finance of both DuPont and General Motors in 1918. He had engineered DuPont's ownership of 43 Percent of GM, purchased from the financially troubled William C. Durant.

He created the General Motors Acceptance Corporation, which provided credit for customers who bought cars on installment. Raskob stayed with GM and DuPont until 1928 when he resigned in a dispute with GM Chairman Alfred P. Sloan. He sold his GM stock and used the proceeds to build the Empire State Building.

Raskob had thirteen children. He died in Wilmington, Delaware in 1950.

Redstone, Sumner Murray
1923-

Sumner Redstone is an outstanding salesman. He has a determination to be number one in everything he does. He survived a fire in 1979 when he was 56 years old. He was dangling high above the ground of Boston's Copley Plaza Hotel and he suffered severe burns on his hands and arms. The tenacity and determination which helped him get through that experience drove him to become one of the most successful and wealthiest giants in America. He has built a $48 billion dollar communications empire.

Redstone expanded his family's drive-in theater chain into many indoor multiplex screens. By 1986 he had built National Amusements into the fifth largest theater chain. He then made a hostile takeover of Viacom. He accepted a great deal of debt. The gamble paid off. Viacom's MTV and Nickelodeon became dominant cable networks for young and teenage audiences.

From this base Redstone bought Paramount Communications. He now owned MTV, Nickelodeon, Showtime, USA Network, Paramount Pictures, Spelling Entertainment, Simon & Schuster, Blockbuster, etc.

Redstone's goal is to be number one. He remains active. He plays tennis, and does 3 miles a day on a treadmill. He has a bowl of oatmeal for lunch. He is not finished. Number one is beckoning.

Rensselaer, Stephen Van
1754-1839

Stephen Van Rensselaer was the last patroon. He was given extensive empires under Dutch rule. He controlled one million acres of New York State. In 1835 he was second only to John Jacob Astor as the richest man in America.

Van Rensselaer had 60,000 to 100,000 tenants living on his estate. He was a Major General in the State Militia. He led a troop of 6,000 men during the War of 1812. The soldiers stationed on the Niagara made an attack on the Canadian shore, but the attack failed when many refused to cross the river. Van Rensselaer was defeated, and he resigned his commission.

In 1824, Van Rensselaer founded the Rensselaer Polytechnic Institute in Troy, New York. It was one of the first schools to teach civilians mechanical arts such as Chemistry, Natural History, and Agriculture.

Van Rensselaer was so lax in collecting rents that at his death the tenants owed him more than $400,000. Less than fifty years after his death, his entire estate, nearly a million acres at its peak, was in the hands of strangers.

Revson, Charles Haskel
1906-1975

Starting as a textile buyer and manager for a nail polish manufacturer in New York City with a borrowed $300, his brother Joseph and a chemist named Charles R. Lachman, Charles Revson formed the Revlon Nail Enamel Corporation. Lachman cooked up a batch of nail enamel and Revson sold $60,000 worth of his new product.

In 1955 Revlon went public at $12 a share. Seventeen years later each share was worth $420, and Revson's holdings were valued at more than $100 million. Eventually, the $300 of borrowed money was built into a conglomerate with annual sales of $400 million in more than eighty countries.

Rhea, Robert
1896-1939

Robert Rhea was the third important member of the triumvirate who refined the Dow Theory and updated and defined it into a systematic guide to the stock market.

Rhea was confined to bed as an invalid for ten years. He made exhaustive studies of the Dow's action and became firmly convinced that it was the only sure method of forecasting stock market movements.

He converted Charles Dow's abstract ideas and William Hamilton's applications into "a manual for those wishing to use it as an aid in speculation."

Rhea's idols were Dow and Hamilton. His devotion to their theory gave his broken life a purpose, and his contribution was a valuable addition to the story of the Dow Theory.

He was born in Nashville Tennessee in 1896. He recovered from tuberculosis only to suffer an airplane crash in 1917. The result was that Rhea was bedridden, and an invalid for the rest of his life.

Richardson, Sid Williams
1891-1959

Sid Williams Richardson was a Texas businessman and philanthropist. He is identified with Fort Worth. With borrowed money, he and Clint Murchison made $1 million dollars in 1919 and 1920. Their fortune waned until business boomed in 1933.

Richardson was a collector of Western Art, especially Remington and Russell. His collection is open to the public since 2006 in the Sid Richardson Museum.

Richardson was a bachelor and upon his death in 1968 he left several million dollars to his nephew-partner Perry Bass. John B. Connolly, the future Governor of Texas was co-executor of the estate, which provided him with steady income for years thereafter.

Riklis, Meshulam
1923-

Meshulam Riklis was born in Odessa and grew up in pre-Israel Tel Aviv. He was a descendant of the Baal-Shemtov, the founder in 18th century Poland of the ultra-orthodox Jewish sect called Hasidim.

Riklis served in the British army during World War II and lived with his bride in a Kibbutz. He came to the United States in 1947, graduated from Ohio State University in 1950, and then moved to Minneapolis. There he taught Hebrew at night and worked as a stock salesman for a local brokerage firm. He was a success with the rich Jews of Minneapolis who financed his independent ventures.

He formed Rapid-American which controlled McCrory Stores, a retail store chain, and Glen Alden, a consumer products company. Riklis controlled a conglomerate with sales of $1.7 billion. It included International Playtex, B.V.D., Schenley Industries, Lerner Shops, and RKO-Stanley Warner Theatres. He used his Jewish identity to advantage and it could be said that he was the first Borscht-Belt entertainer to rule an American business empire. He deserves his place in our business history.

The Robber Barons

Many men were prominent throughout the history of our country's financial development. The Rockefellers with Standard Oil controlled enormous amounts of capital and were earning $60 million a year At the turn of the century John D. was worth $1 billion. James Keene was quoted as saying "I can see no stopping them. They will own the country in a few years." The great quartet of the Southwest, Collis Huntington, Mark Hopkins, Leland Stanford, and Charles Crocker achieved a monopoly of incalculable value with millions of acres of mineral-rich western land. Nothing could check the hegemony of the quartet over the west coast. Jay Cooke, the financier who personally managed the Civil War debt, Cyrus McCormick who invented the Reaper, Philip Armour who founded a meatpacking dynasty—both helped build Chicago and the Midwest.

The greatest of the "Robber Barons" were an unhappy lot, making money and too absorbed to do anything else. They would have no friends or enjoy life as normal people know it. They were great silent men with little to talk about or think about except their business operations. Their greed and ambition knew no bounds, for money and power was the game. In that fabulous era of our country's development, with their daring, their vision, their imagination, their overweening desire to outdo each other and dominate their industry and their enemies, they succeeded in building the greatest industrial nation in the world. It is for this fact alone that we owe them thanks, and can forgive the selfish motives that drove them to their success.

Rockefeller, John Davison
1839-1937

The rise of John D. Rockefeller and the Standard Oil Trust was a phenomenon unmatched in American financial history, but one which proved that happiness is only a dream. Rockefeller is quoted as saying, "It is wrong to assume that men of immense wealth are always happy." Perhaps the feud and bitter rivalry between the houses of Morgan and Rockefeller caused them both unhappiness. They both had immense wealth and were haters. The Standard Oil Trust eclipsed J.P. Morgan's holdings when it controlled the National City Bank and had far more assets than any bank in the country. The ambitious Morgan couldn't stand that, but his formation of United States Steel should have satisfied his giant ego.

John D. Rockefeller grew up in western New York and later near Cleveland. He was one of five children in a struggling family. He was harshly disciplined, quiet, shy, reserved, and serious. He received only a few years of poor schooling. In Cleveland he studied bookkeeping for a year.

Initially Rockefeller owned refineries that developed kerosene which sold for twice as much as a barrel of crude. In 1870, he reorganized the Standard Oil Company of Ohio with $1,000,000 in capital. It was the world's largest oil manufacturing concern. In 1872, about 80 percent of the other Cleveland refiners sold out, mostly for cash. By 1880, anti-monopoly legislation broke up the Standard Oil Trust into twenty companies. However, the trust was then replaced –The Standard Oil Company of New Jersey was formed as a holding company to own and control the various Standard subsidiaries.

Rogers, Henry Huttleston
1840-1909

Henry Rogers became a partner of John D. Rockefeller and built a fortune of $100 million at Standard Oil. Rogers initiated the concept of pipelines to transport oil. He branched out into gas, copper, steel, banking, railroad, and insurance.

Rogers was a tall, handsome man. He was witty, charming, and generous in his private life. He was merciless in business.

Rogers died in 1907 at the age of 69. He had four children with his first wife and four with his second wife, after his first wife died. His eldest son, Henry H. Rogers II took charge of the family holdings after his father's death.

Romney, Willard Mitt
1947-

Mitt Romney is an American businessman who was the Republican nominee for President of the United States in 2012. He lost to Barack Obama, who won reelection and gained a second term as president. Romney was the 70th Governor of Massachusetts.

Romney was raised in Michigan. His father, George also ran for president, and lost when he used the term "brainwashed" in connection to the Vietnam War. Mitt and his wife Ann have five children. He went to Brigham Young and Harvard. In 1977 he secured a position at Bain & company. Later, as CEO of Bain he spun off Bain Capital, and it became a highly profitable private equity investment firm. It was the largest of its kind in the United States. Romney's net worth in 2012 was estimated at $190 to $250 million.

Rosenwald, Julius
1862-1932

Julius Rosenwald went to Chicago as a young man and bought a small mail-order house called Sears, Roebuck & Company. When he wanted money to expand he approached his "cousin" Henry Goldman. He asked Goldman for a loan of five million dollars.

Goldman and Philip Lehman offered Rosenwald a better suggestion. Why not make a public offering of Sears stock and make ten million dollars. The foundation of a gigantic mail-order house was thereby laid.

Rothschild Family
Mayer Amschel Rothschild   1744-1812

The House of Rothschild is a European banking dynasty that was founded by Nathan Mayer Rothschild in Germany. He was born in 1777.

Following Napoleon's defeat at Waterloo the Rothschild family had complete control of the British economy. The Rothschild's are known for their charitable work and as winemakers. The Rothschild interests were represented in America by August Belmont.

Rukeyser, Louis Richard "Lou"
1933-2006

Lou Rukeyser was an American financial journalist, columnist, commentator, and author. He contributed through print, radio, and television.

Rukeyser is best known and remembered for his role as host of Wall Street Week, which appeared every Friday night on PBS. He was born in New York City and graduated from New Rochelle High School in 1950. He went on to Princeton University's Woodrow Wilson School of Public and International Affairs, where he graduated in 1954.

After eleven years as a foreign correspondent for the Baltimore Sun, Lou joined ABC and moved to television and continued to write for newspapers as a syndicated columnist. In 1970 he started the Public Broadcasting Service (PBS) Series, Wall Street Week. Rukeyser made the stock market and the economy better known to the public for 32 years.

As competition increased by CNBC and others, network executives wanted to replace Rukeyser with younger hosts. He was 69 and they wanted higher ratings. In his final episode, Rukeyser urged viewers to write PBS stations and ask for the new show he would create. Maryland Public Television fired him immediately after the broadcast and erased the master tape.

Rukeyser was soon diagnosed with Multiple Myeloma (a type of bone cancer). He died at his Greenwich, Connecticut home in 2006. He was survived by his wife Alexandra Gill and their daughters Beverley, Susan, and Stacy.

Russell, Richard

Richard Russell is Charles Dow's foremost modern disciple. He's a worthy successor to William P. Hamilton and Robert Rhea. He believes that it is his duty to the mass of investors to prove its validity.

The popularity of the Dow Jones Industrial Average is supreme. Talleyrand once said, "Everybody knows more than anybody." Russell claims that this maxim is the essence of the Dow Theory. The combined investments of all the people who are in the stock market determine the direction of prices.

The term "Dow Theory" was coined in 1902 by S.A. Nelson. The whole theory is contained in the articles Charles H. Dow wrote for the Wall Street Journal in 1901 and 1902. Dow never wrote a formal book on his theories. It remained for William P. Hamilton to succeed him at the journal and expand on his ideas. The Dow Theory is not infallible, but it is considered by many market followers to be the most reliable barometer of stock trends and the economy.

Ryan, Thomas Fortune
1851-1928

Thomas Ryan was a dominant force in New York transit. He was born in 1851 on a small farm in Virginia. At the age of 21 in 1872, he moved to New York City. He became a messenger in a Wall Street firm. With his father-in-law's help he became a partner in his own brokerage firm and bought a seat on the stock exchange.

He developed power in New York and had great connections in Tammany Hall. Ryan then out-bribed all opposition to become owner of the Broadway franchise for the Metropolitan Traction Company. He acquired new rail lines and also entered banking, utilities, and tobacco.

In 1904 Ryan bought Washington Life Insurance Company and then took control of Equitable. Scandals dogged Ryan at every turn, but he always was able to avoid any financial or criminal actions.

Ryan retired to his Fifth Avenue mansion. His personal life was unconstrained. When his wife died in 1917 he was 66. He married two weeks later and his eldest son Allan called his father's speedy marriage "disgraceful." This earned him his father's anger and he was cut out of his will. Ryan died in 1928 at the age of 77. His estate of about $200 million was carved into 54 pieces with six children and many grandchildren.

Sachs, Joseph

Joseph Sachs was a poor Bavarian saddle-maker who grew up near Wurzburg. He was hired as a tutor and fell in love with Sophia Baer. Her parents disapproved of Joseph, so they eloped to Rotterdam and were married in 1848. They boarded a ship bound for America, and landed in Baltimore.

Joseph worked as a school teacher and as a Rabbi in Baltimore and Boston before settling in New York. Sachs and Goldman were friends and their oldest son Julius married the Goldman's daughter Rosa. In the 1880s Sophia's second son Sam was matched up with another Goldman daughter, Louisa. Marcus Goldman invited Sam to be his first partner in the commercial-paper business.

Marcus Goldman loaned Sam $15,000 which was to be paid back in three promissory notes of $5,000 each. After paying two of the notes, Sam's son Walter was born. Marcus wrote Sam that in honor of his "energy and ability" as a partner he was forgiving him the final payment.

It was only natural that time passed, and the firm of Goldman Sachs grew into a powerful force in the financial world. It remains so today.

Sage, Russell
1816-1906

Russell Sage was a wholesale grocer from Troy, New York. He was born in 1816. While serving as a town Alderman and Treasurer he seized control of a local railroad. He paid $200,000 for it and sold it to New York Central for almost $1,000,000. Chicanery and bribery were to be Sage's method of success during his long career. He was elected to Congress in 1854.

After several successful railroad deals, Sage met Jay Gould. He became known as the "put and call king" because he used options to buy and sell stocks. He made a sizeable fortune during the Civil War.

Sage was one of the smartest Robber Barons because he was out of the public view for most of his career.

Sanders, Harland David "Colonel"
1890-1980

Harland David Sanders was born on a farm in Indiana in 1890. His father died when he was five years old. He had a hard life and dropped out of school in the sixth grade. Sanders had many jobs and lost most of them because of his bad temper. He needed to get his own business so nobody could fire him.

He opened a gas station and served meals to his customers. In the late 1930s he bought a pressure cooker from a salesman who came into his store one day. It cut the cooking time and he didn't have to prepare the food so far ahead. Customers raved about his chicken, and in 1952 he settled on his mixture of 11 herbs and spices. Sanders' café was a great success. He expanded his seating to 142. He received a Colonel's Commission from the Governor of Kentucky. From that time on he referred to himself as Colonel Sanders. In 1949 he married Claudia Leddington who worked for him since 1932. He divorced Josephine two years earlier after a long and unhappy marriage that included the death of their only son, Harland Jr. who was just 19.

Colonel Sanders' Kentucky Fried Chicken grew through franchising to more than 2,000 outlets by the end of 1960, and he added 100 more outlets by 1963. John Brown Jr. was the son of a long-time friend. He offered to buy Sanders' franchise business. In February, 1964 Sanders sold Kentucky Fried Chicken to Brown and a partner, Jack Massey, for $2 million. In 1966 KFC had $15 million in sales. The company went public in 1966. In 1969 it was listed on the New York Stock Exchange. In 1970, the company had 3,000 outlets in 48 countries. By 1997 that figure was up to 10,000 stores in 76 countries.

In 1971, John Brown sold out to Heublein, Inc., which was acquired by R.J. Reynolds Industries (RJR Nabisco). In 1986, Pepsico bought KFC for about $840 million. In 1997, Pepsico spun off Taco Bell, Pizza Hut, and KFC into an independent restaurant company called Tri-Con Global Restaurants, Inc.. They have a total of about 30,000 outlets in 100 countries.

Saunders, Clarence
1881-1953

Clarence Saunders was an American grocer who was the first to develop the modern retail sales model of self-service. His ideas had a great influence on the development of the modern supermarket.

Sunders developed an automated store and incorporated it in his Piggly Wiggly chain. He was born in Virginia and left school at 14 to clerk in a general store. When he was 19 he was earning $30 a month as a salesman for a wholesale grocer. In 1902 he formed a wholesale cooperative in Memphis. In 1915 he organized Saunders-Blackburn Co., a wholesale grocer which sold for cash only.

In 1916, Saunders launched the self-service revolution in the USA by opening the first Piggly Wiggly in Memphis, Tennessee. Customers paid cash and selected their own goods from the shelves. The self-service store was patented by Saunders in 1917. By 1922, after only six years, Piggly Wiggly had grown to 1,200 stores in 29 states. By 1932, the chain had grown to 2,660 stores doing over $180 million annually.

Saunders listed Piggly Wiggly on the New York Stock Exchange. Unfortunately, a group of franchisees failed, and a bear raid caused the stock to fall. Saunders borrowed $10 million and cornered the stock. He owned 196,000 of the 200,000 shares. The price rose from 39 in 1922 to 124 in March, 1923. The bears poured in the shares and the price was driven back down. Saunders had to sell his stock at a loss, which cost him $3 million, forcing him into bankruptcy. Afterwards, Saunders had no further association with the company.

Schiff, Jacob H.
1847-1920

Jacob H. Schiff joined the firm of Kuhn, Loeb & Co. It was the company of his father-in-law, Solomon Loeb. Once he joined the firm, it began to play a major role in American financial capitalism. Schiff was brought up in the German Financial Capital of Frankfurt am Main. He came to New York after the Civil War, in 1866.

Schiff's contacts in Europe were crucial. He was attracted to railroads. By 1885, when he was 38, he became head of the firm. He helped capitalize more than twelve railroads. By 1900 Kuhn, Loeb & Co. engaged in capitalizing almost all types of American industry.

When United States Steel was launched, the syndicate was paid 1,300,000 shares by J.P. Morgan. When the issue was distributed on the open market, the syndicate made a profit of $5,800,000. Such was the lucrative profits that can be made in investment banking.

Jacob Schiff was a principle of the "giants' who were involved in the corner of the Northern Pacific which was responsible for the Panic of 1901. Schiff and Ned Harriman were locked in a battle to control Northern Pacific with James Hill and J.P. Morgan. The four giants resolved their differences by joining in the ownership of Northern Securities set up by Morgan. Their egos were finally satisfied and the financial panic was history.

Schultz, Howard
1953-

Brooklyn-born Howard Schultz has truly lived the American dream. He was poor, growing up in the projects of Brooklyn, but he had what it takes to succeed.

Howard worked for a small company called Starbucks. On a business trip to Italy he was impressed with the way Italians sat over their cups of Espresso, and he was determined to bring the romance of Italian Espresso bars to America.

Howard left Starbucks to strike out on his own, and opened a couple of Espresso bars called "Il Giornale." With the help of a few investors Schultz merged which Starbucks which had six outlets. After one year Starbucks had 11 stores. When he left his job as CEO in 2000 to become Chairman, Schultz had built Starbucks into a company that had annual revenues of nearly 2 billion dollars.

When Howard returned as CEO Starbucks was a $10 billion dollar company. He closed 600 underperforming stores and took a $340 million dollar charge. Most of the stores he closed were only open for three years or less.

Many analysts in the media had written Starbucks' obituary, but Howard Schultz had known hard times growing up in Brooklyn. He loved what he was doing. Fear of failure is a great motivator. Starbucks is back and flourishing with the guidance of the man who gave birth to it.

Schwarzman, Stephen Allen (Steve)
1947-

Steve Schwarzman is an American financier and philanthropist. He is Chairman, CEO, and co-founder of the Blackstone Group, a private equity firm.

Schwarzman was born in Pennsylvania. His father owned a dry-goods store in Philadelphia. Steve went to Yale University and belonged to the Skull and Bones Society with George W. Bush. He graduated in 1969. He then went on to the Harvard Business School and graduated in 1972.

After a stint at DLJ (Donaldson, Lufkin, Jenrette) Schwarzman started working at Lehman Brothers. He was Managing Director at age 31. He eventually became the head of Global Mergers and Acquisitions. In 1985 Steve and his boss Peter Peterson started Blackstone.

Schwarzman lives at 740 Park Avenue in a large apartment that he bought from Saul Steinberg in 2000 for about 30 million dollars.

When Blackstone went public in 2007, it was revealed that Schwarzman earned about $398.3 million in fiscal 2006. He also received $684 million, selling part of his Blackstone stake in the IPO, keeping the balance which was then worth $9.1 billion. Steve gave $100 million to the New York Public Library which named the building after him. He is married to his second wife. He has two children from his first marriage and a step-child from his second wife's first marriage.

Schwarzman's net worth is estimated at $4.7 billion by Forbes in 2011.

Sears, Richard
1863-1914

Richard Sears was a railroad station agent in Minnesota. He started a business selling watches through mail order catalogues. He moved to Chicago where he met Alvah C. Roebuck who joined him in the business. In 1897, the corporate name became Sears, Roebuck & Co.

The first Sears catalogue was published in 1888. By 1894 it had grown to 322 pages featuring sewing machines, bicycles, sporting goods, automobiles, and other items. Julius Rosenwald, a clothing manufacturer became a partner in 1895. Alvah Roebuck resigned due to ill health.

Sales were $400,000 in 1893 and $750,000 two years later. In the 1970s Roebuck was dropped from the name of the stock. The company was the largest retailer in the United States until the early 1960s. Sears added insurance with the Allstate Insurance Company in 1971. During the Mid -Twentieth- Century it added Dean Witter and Coldwell Banker Real Estate. In 1986, it introduced The Discover Card in 1985.

In the 1990s, the company began disposing of many of its non-retail entities. In 2004, Sears merged with K-Mart investor Edward Lampert who was interested in the company becoming an investment company rather than a retailer.

Seligman, Jesse
1819-1880

Jesse Seligman agreed to go out West and open a store in San Francisco during the gold rush. The cups and pans which cost pennies back East were selling for five to ten dollars. Eventually, the man's went into banking. They were the only bankers who did not close their doors during The Panic of 1857.

Jesse was a great friend of Ulysses S. Grant, and during The Civil War the Seligmans sold over $60 million worth of Federal Securities. At the war's end Joseph Seligman brought the brothers together to organize the International House of Seligman. The House of Seligman was a copy of The House of Rothschild. J. & W. Seligman & Company was officially born and each brother was given an assignment suitable to his temperament and talent.

Seligman, House of

Within hours of Robert E. Lee's surrender, Joseph Seligman put his plan to work. He summoned his brothers together to organize The International House of Seligman. The house would span the American continent and cover the whole of Europe. Each of the eight brothers would be given an assignment based on his temperament and his talent. William was placed in charge of Paris, Henry, who remained in Germany longest was given Frankfurt. Isaac was assigned to London, Joseph, Jesse, and James remained in New York. Abraham and Leopold were sent to San Francisco. The House of Seligman was a copy of The House of Rothschild.

Now that the war was over, The Seligman's opened another office in New Orleans. In a remarkable feat of diplomacy, Joseph Seligman invited General Ulysses S. Grant, Commander of the Northwest forces, and Brigadier Pierre Gustine Beauregard, former Commander of the Southern Army of the Potomac to dinner. They chatted amiably, played snooker in the billiard room, and strolled arm-in-arm through the garden as Joseph Seligman looked on in satisfaction.

Singer, Isaac Merrit
1811-1875

Isaac Singer built a sturdy sewing machine that was operated by a foot treadle. He marketed it aggressively. Elias Howe filed suit for infringement of his patents. Howe won the suit in 1854 and collected royalties from Singer. Howe became wealthy, getting $4,000 a week in royalty fees.

Singer built the business to major proportions, bringing the machine within reach of the poor by installment sales. His motto was, "a machine in every home."

Slater, Samuel
1758-1835

Samuel Slater was an apprentice in England for a partner of Arkwright who invented a machine for ribbed stockings. He thought that the prospects for the textile business were much better in America.

Slater went to work for Moses Brown in Rhode Island. Brown had a spinning mill. Within a year, in a mill owned by Ezekiel Carpenter, Slater constructed three carding machines, a spinning frame with 72 spindles, and other needed equipment.

The 1810 census showed 1,776 wool-carding machines. By the end of The War of 1812 woolen mills employed 40,000 people. Slater built a fortune of $500,000, but he remained a frugal man.

Smith, Cyrus R.
1889-1990

American Airlines grew out of a 1934 reorganization of the struggling little American Airways. Cyrus R. Smith was named its first President. Smith ran the company well enough to move ahead of its competition in 1939.

Right after the war, Smith took a gamble and ordered $80 million dollars worth of new equipment to replace his entire fleet of smaller aircraft. The fifty-two passenger DC-6s and forty passenger Convair 240s led American Airlines to a profit in 1950 of $10.4 million on total revenues of $119 million.

Smith, Fred
1944-

Fred Smith had a great pedigree. Both his grandfather and father ran transportation companies. He was destined to be a leader and an entrepreneur. He faced tragedy early in his life when his father died. He was only four. He also contracted a disease that put him on crutches for more than two years when he was eight. Smith went to Yale and joined The Platoon Leader Training Program of the U.S. Marines. He also wrote a 15 page report for a term paper in Economics, which turned out to be a blueprint for Federal Express. When he graduated from Yale in 1966, he joined the Marines. His father and three uncles had served in the military. Fred Smith served two tours of duty in Vietnam. He was a company commander and earned two Purple Hearts. Smith flew more than two tours of duty in Vietnam.

It turned out that his leadership experience, the training, discipline, etc. that he absorbed as a Marine Captain would stick with him all his life, and prepare him for the future. He founded Federal Express with his $4 million dollar inheritance and lost $27 million in the first two years. The company was on the verge of bankruptcy. He renegotiated his bank loans and kept the company afloat. In 1978, Fed Ex went public. Today Fed Ex is a global transportation company that does $38 billion a year in revenues and employs nearly 300,000 people and delivers millions of shipments a day in 22 countries.

Sobel, Robert
1931-1999

Robert Sobel was a professor of history at Hofstra University. He was a well-known and prolific writer of business histories.

Sobel was born in The Bronx, in New York City. He went to City College of New York where he obtained a BSS and MA degree. After a stint in the U.S. Army, he earned a PhD. from New York University in 1957.

Sobel's first major work was "The Big Board"- a History of The New York Stock Exchange" In 1965. He went on to write 30 more books. His passion was Wall Street. His books about Wall Street were his mission in life. Among the many great works Robert Sobel wrote were the following:

Panic on Wall Street.
The Great Bull Market.
The Curbstone Brokers.
The Entrepreneurs.
The Manipulators.
Inside Wall Street.
The Last Bull Market.
The New Game on Wall Street.

As a personal note, this author is eternally grateful that Bob Sobel agreed to write the Foreword to my analytical bibliography, "Best Books on the Stock Market." The book won the American Library Association's award as the best book in finance. I knew even early in his career that Robert Sobel would add many important works to the literature of Wall Street.

Solomon, Haym
1740-1785

Haym Solomon contributed $800,000 of his own funds to the Revolutionary War effort. The British sentenced him to be hanged in New York. He fled to Philadelphia in 1778, leaving behind his entire fortune and his young family. He saved the Continental Army on more than one occasion.

Haym Solomon received an urgent request from Washington on Yom Kippur. Washington needed $500,000 to keep the Army afloat. In one night, Solomon raised the funds. He played a crucial role in the success of the Revolution.

Solomon died poor and his heirs never received any part of the hundreds of thousands of dollars he advanced for the war effort.

Sperry, Elmer Ambrose
1850-1930

Elmer Sperry was a famous inventor who had taken out nearly 400 patents, about twice the number taken out by Thomas Edison.

He is best known for his Sperry Gyroscope for the utilization of ships, airplanes, and aerial torpedoes.

Elmer Ambrose Sperry was born in Cortland, New York in 1860. He was the son of Stephen Decatur and Mary Sperry. He attended Cornell University for one term from 1879 to 1880.

He was survived by two sons who lived in Brooklyn, New York. He died at St. John's Hospital in Brooklyn from complications of a gallstone operation. He was seventy years old.

Spreckels, Claus
1828-1928

Claus Spreckels was "Sugar King of the West." When the 18 year old Spreckels immigrated to America from Hanover, Germany in 1846, he started working in the grocery business in South Carolina. He met his wife and bought the grocery store, sold it, and opened a retail store in New York City. In 1856, Spreckels followed the gold rush to California, where he opened a grocery and retail store in San Francisco.

Spreckels then created a sugar business, The Bay Sugar Refining Company, tapping the supply of sugar cane from Hawaii. After selling his business, Spreckels spent the next two years in Europe studying all phases of sugar production. He returned to California in 1867, and built the largest sugar refinery on the Pacific Coast. Five years later the plant was processing more than 50 million pounds of sugar per year.

Spreckels bought a mansion on Fifth Avenue in 1906. He died two years later at the age of eighty, leaving a fortune estimated at $50 million. His son lost most of his $50 million dollar fortune in the stock market crash of 1929.

Stanford, Leland
1824-1893

Leland Stanford was one of the builders of the West. He was born in New York, but was Governor of California. Stanford drove the Golden Spike that connected the first transcontinental railroad in 1869.

In 1885, he defeated George Hearst for the U.S. Senate and went to Washington. Stanford will be remembered along with Mark Hopkins, Charles Crocker, and Collis Huntington as the four men who pioneered the building of California. The four partners, led by Huntington and Stanford became the dominant force in Western business. Stanford was credited with keeping the state loyal to the union during the Civil War.

Stanford is best known for founding one of the nation's most prominent universities. He bequeathed thirty million dollars to found Stanford University in memory of his only son and namesake who died of Typhoid Fever in 1884 at the age of fifteen. He also donated land for the campus on his ranch at Palo Alto.

Steinberg, Saul Philip
1939-

Brooklyn-born Saul Steinberg went to The Wharton School of Finance. He believed that IBM's method of doing business was an opportunity to make a lot of money. He leased IBM computers long-term. Not only did he recover the cost of the computer, but he could sell or lease the computer after the initial lease expired.

Leasco gave birth to a new industry---computer leasing. The growth of his company allowed Steinberg to buy several small companies. Subsequently, Steinberg bought Reliance Insurance Company, an old Philadelphia-based Fire and Casualty Underwriter, which had more than $100 million in redundant capital. But this is not the way Steinberg will be remembered.

At the tender age of twenty-nine Steinberg set his sights on the $9 billion dollar Chemical Bank. He was invading the establishment. Management of the Chemical Bank fought back, and after months of intrigue, Saul Steinberg withdrew his interest in acquiring the Chemical Bank.

Stewart, Alexander Turney
1803-1876

A.T. Stewart is credited with founding the first department store in the United States. He was born in Belfast, Ireland. His father died shortly after he was born. His grandfather wanted him to enter the ministry, but at seventeen, Stewart left school and went to New York City. He taught Ancient History at a private school and he inherited $5,000, which he used to buy Irish lace and linens, which he sold in New York.

In 1813, he opened a small dry-goods store on Lower Broadway. He and his wife lived above the store. He sent $50,000 worth of clothing to the victims of The Chicago Fire. He also supplied uniforms and blankets to Union troops at cost. Stewart was a shrewd dealer. He was tough with his employees, but fawned over his customers. He used display windows to show his merchandise. He owned factories that supplied his stores.

Stewart built a huge building near City Hall. He then built a larger store at Ninth Street and Broadway. It was the largest retail store in the world. By 1870, Stewart was doing over $10 million a year. Macy's was doing $1 million and Marshall Field $3 million. Stewart built a marble mansion for $1 million at Fifth Avenue and 34th Street. He and his wife moved in when he was sixty-six.

After being turned down for a political job by his friend, President Ulysses S. Grant, Stewart created a beautiful city—Garden City, Long Island. It was intended for working people. Meanwhile, his retail business and real estate holdings made him the richest man in New York. When he died in 1876, 8,000 people attended his funeral. When asked about the secret of his success he replied, "work, work, work!." His fortune was estimated at $50 million.

Straus, Isidor
1845-1912

Isidor Straus was a co-owner of Macy's Department Store with his brother Nathan. He served briefly as a member of the United States House of Representatives. He died with his wife Ida in the sinking of the passenger ship RMS Titanic.

Straus was born in Germany. He was the first of five children of Lazarus Straus (1809-1898) and his second wife Sara (1823-1876). In 1851 his family immigrated to the United States. Lazarus opened a dry-goods store. Isidor volunteered to serve in the Confederate Army but was turned down. There were not arms enough to equip the men. He was too young. His father served in the 4th Georgia Regiment. Isidor earned $12,000 in gold trading in Confederate bonds.

Following the war Lazarus and Isidor formed L. Straus & Sons, importers of crockery, china, and porcelain. In 1874, Nathan convinced Rowland H. Macy to allow L. Straus & Sons to open a crockery department in the basement of his store. By 1896, the Straus Brothers had gained full ownership of R.H. Macy & Co.

Isidor and his wife Ida refused a seat on a lifeboat and died arm in arm when the RMS Titanic sank after hitting an iceberg on April 15, 1912.

Straus, Lazarus
1809-1878

The patriarch of the Straus Family was Lazarus Straus. He was an immigrant from Bavaria. He arrived in the United States in 1852 and started to make his fortune as a peddler. He opened a general store in Georgia, where he lived until the Civil War.

After a brief stay in Philadelphia, Lazarus moved to New York. He founded a business in wholesale china and glassware in 1866. His sons Isidor and Nathan were active in the business. Nathan had frequent dealings with Rowland Macy who granted Lazarus Straus & Sons the concession for their china and glass departments.

The concession was so successful that a Macy's partner, Webster sold his entire interest in Macy's to Isidor and Nathan in 1896 for $1,200,000, which gave the Straus sons control of the whole business. By 1900, sales at Macy's reached $10 million. Lazarus died in 1898 and Isidor died in the Titanic disaster in 1912

Strauss, Levi
1829-1902

Levi Strauss was a German-born American businessman who founded the first company to manufacture blue jeans. His firm, Levi Strauss & Co. began in 1853 in San Francisco, California.

Strauss was born in Bavaria, Germany. He sailed for the United States at 18. Levi was chosen by his family to open a West Coast branch dry-goods store.

In 1872, Jacob Davis, a Reno, Nevada tailor started making men's work pants with metal points of strain for greater strength. He needed a partner, so he turned to Levi Strauss, from whom he purchased his fabric. In 1873, Strauss and Davis received a patent for using copper rivets to strengthen the pockets of denim work pants.

Levi Strauss died in 1902 at the age of 73. He never married. He left the business to his four nephews. He left bequests to both the Hebrew and Catholic Orphan Asylums. Levi's fortune was around $6 million dollars, ($158 million in 2012 dollars).

Swope, Gerard
1872-1957

When Gerard Swope retired from General Electric's Presidency in 1939, its sales had reached $342 million, far too great an operation to be kept in one man's mind, unless the mind were as agile and retentive as that of a Swope.

But, he also possessed the acumen to recognize that with more growth in sight, a major corporate overhaul was going to be necessary, and Swope groomed Charles E. Wilson ("Electric Charlie") to distinguish him from G.M.'s ("Engine Charlie") for the post.

Taylor, Moses
1806-1882

Moses Taylor was President of The National City Bank of New York. He was a clerk for an importer at the age of fifteen. Then he started a company importing Cuban sugar. A year after he set up the business, his store was destroyed by the great fire of 1835. Two years later, the Panic of 1837 shook many businesses, but Taylor continued to grow.

Taylor bought control of The Delaware, Lackawanna & Western Railroad for $5 a share. Seven years later, the stock soared to $240 per share. In 1837, Taylor was elected to the Board of Directors of City Bank. In 1856, he was named President of the bank, renamed The National City Bank. By the time of his death in 1882, the bank had assets of more than $16 million.

Taylor became interested in railroads. He knew Commodore Vanderbilt and sold his stock to him. He also financed Cyrus Field who laid the first Atlantic Telegraph Cable from Valencia, Ireland to Trinity Bay, Newfoundland. The project went from near collapse to ultimate success.

At his death, Taylor left a fortune of between $40 and $50 million to his wife Catherine and their five children.

Thornton, Charles B. "Tex"
1913-1981

"Tex Thornton was a full Colonel at the age of twenty-eight. He left Ford in 1948 to join Hughes Aircraft as a Vice-President. In 1953, along with Roy L. Ash and Hugh Jameson, Thornton took over Litton when Charles Litton was retiring. Litton took $1 million in cash rather than stock in the new Litton Industries.

The company earned $154,000 on sales of $3 million in the first nine months. Four years later, sales had reached nearly $100 million and net profits were almost $4 million. By then Litton had done 17 mergers.

By 1970, Litton reported earnings of $69 million on sales of $2.4 billion.

Tiffany, Charles L.
1812-1902

Charles L. Tiffany opened his first store with a loan of $1,000 from his father. After three days, he had earned $498. Today Tiffany's serves the wealthy and powerful of the world.

When Charles Tiffany died in 1902 at the age of ninety, he was survived by four of his six children. Tiffany's is the premier jeweler in America. After a management buyout and public offering in 1984, Tiffany's began a rapid expansion. By 1994, there were eighty-four stores in fourteen countries, with revenues of more than $682 million.

Tisch, Lawrence, Alan "Larry"
1923-2003

Larry Tisch was a Wall Street investor and self-made billionaire. He was CEO of CBS Television Network from 1986 to 1995. He and his brother Bob Tisch owned The Loew's Corporation.

Tisch was born in Brooklyn in 1923. He was the son of Russian immigrants Sadye and Al Tisch. His father was an All-American basketball player at The City University of New York and owned two summer camps.

Larry Tisch graduated from New York University and received an MBA from The Wharton School. His first investment was a 300 room hotel in Lakewood, New Jersey for $125,000. What followed was the purchase of a dozen hotels in Atlantic City and the Catskills.

In 1960, using the proceeds of his hotels, Tisch gained control of Loew's Theatres, a large movie house chain. Bob and Larry Tisch would later tear down many of the theatres to build apartments and hotels making millions in profits.

The Tisch brothers soon diversified the business, successfully entering a variety of areas. In 1968, Loew's acquired Lorillard, the 5th largest tobacco company in the U.S. at the time, which owned the popular brands Kent, Newport, and True. In 1974, they bought a nearly bankrupt insurance company, CNA Financial Corporation. They also purchased The Bulova Watch Company.

Tisch built Loew's into a highly profitable conglomerate with 14 hotels, 67 movie theaters, CNA Financial, Bulova, and Lorillard, with revenues of $100 million in 1970, increasing to more than $3 billion in 1980.

In 2002, the year before Larry's death, the corporation had revenues of more than $17 billion and assets of more than $70 billion.

Trippe, Juan Terry
1899-1981

A year after he graduated from Yale, Juan Trippe and his friend John Hambleton bought nine Navy flying boats for $4,500. They were about to be junked. Trippe and his friend scraped up enough cash to found Eastern Air Transport. Eastern merged with Colonial Airways to become Colonial Air Transport, which started to carry New York to Boston mail. Charles Lindbergh was flying mail from St. Louis to Chicago.

Lindbergh's flight across the Atlantic sparked increased interest in Wall Street. This led to the formation of United, TWA, and American Airlines. Trippe's Pan American Airways looked beyond the limits of the continental United States. Pan Am serviced the Philippines, Macao and Hong Kong, and he spanned the Atlantic, and serviced London and Lisbon. To produce planes for the airlines, Martin, Boeing, and Douglas began to gear up production. The Douglas DC3 took to the air in 1936. It turned out to be the workhorse of World War II.

Trump, Donald John Sr.
1946-

Donald Trump is an American business magnate, television personality, and author. He is the Chairman of Trump Entertainment Resorts. Trump is the son of Fred Trump, a wealthy New York City real estate developer. Donald worked with his father while he attended The Wharton School of the University of Pennsylvania. In 1971, he was given control of the company and named it The Trump Organization In 2010. Trump expressed his interest in becoming a candidate for President of the United States in 2012.

Trump's paternal grandparents were German immigrants. His grandfather, Frederick Trump (born Friedrich Trumpf), immigrated to the United States in 1885. At 13 Donald was sent to The New York Military Academy in upstate New York. Trump earned academic honors and played varsity football in 1962, and soccer in 1963, and baseball (captain) in 1964.

Trump is known as The Donald. His first wife was Ivana Trump. He is a golfer and is a member of The Winged Foot Golf Club in Mamaroneck, New York. Trump does not drink alcohol. Melania Knauss is his third wife. They have a son, Barron. There are three children from his first marriage-Donald Jr., Ivanka, and Eric.

After concentrating on his father's middle-class rental housing in Brooklyn, Queens, and Staten Island, Donald Trump zeroed in on Manhattan. He turned the bankrupt Commodore Hotel into a new Grand Hyatt. Trump had a plan to develop the old Penn Central for $60 million with no money down. Trump brokered the development of The Javits Convention Center on property he owned. He estimated that his company could build it for $110 million. It cost the state $450 million. He received a broker's fee.

Trump restored The Wollman Rink in Central Park. He renovated the Trump Tower, and bought the Atlantic City hotels-The Taj Mahal and Resorts International. The Trump story is still unfolding. There are many projects in work, and Donald Trump is a media star with his successful show "The Apprentice."

Tsai, Gerald
1929-2006

Gerald Tsai was born in Shanghai in 1929 to westernized Chinese parents. His father was educated at The University of Michigan. Gerald Tsai went to Wesleyan University and transferred to Boston University.

Tsai found the stock market to his liking. He worked at Fidelity and then Bache & Co. as a stock analyst. At Fidelity he started The Fidelity Capital Fund in 1957. Money poured in because Tsai's performance was spectacular. He bought speculative stocks and his turnover was over 100 percent. By 1965 Gerry Tsai was well known. Tsai's race and national origin added to the mystique of his success.

When it became clear that he couldn't succeed Johnson as Fidelity's leader, Gerry Tsai resigned, sold his Fidelity stock for $2.2 million, and left Boston for New York to organize his own mutual fund. He established his Manhattan Fund, set about selling shares at $10 each. How many shares could be sold before the opening date of February 15, 1966? Tsai set a goal of $25 million. Checks poured in. Could it be $100 million? Harold L. Bache, head of the firm that managed The Manhattan Fund share offering handed Tsai a check for $247 million. Tsai's new organization, Tsai Management and Research started life with an annual gross income of a million and a quarter dollars.

Expectations were so high that failure was inevitable. The market was too high and the bull market of the 1960s had reached a peak that it would not reach again. So Gerry Tsai rode unaware toward his fall and his adoring public toward its disillusionment. Tsai's name remained undimmed. His firm had grown to over $500 million. In August 1968 he sold Tsai Management and Research to CNA Financial Corporation for an executive post and CNA stock worth $30 million. He had a trust fund that could assure his son a considerable income for life.

Turner, Ted
1938-

Rising above the traumatic effects of his father's suicide, Ted Turner has had a sterling career that distinguished him in the annals of entrepreneurship. He was only twenty-four years old.

The tragedy stirred Turner to strive for success. He worked eighteen hours a day. He was an only child. His father had a billboard company.

Ted Turner founded CNN, a cable news channel that was dedicated to 24 hour news. He became a billionaire many times over. After merging with Time Warner, Turner was worth $10 billion. The disaster of merging with AOL caused Turner to lose nearly $10 million a day for two and a half years. All told he lost $7 billion. Still he pledged $1 billion of what was left to the U.N.

Today Ted turner has the largest herd of Bison in the world and is the co-founder of Ted's Montana Grill Restaurant Chain. It has grown to forty-six restaurants in sixteen states.

Untermeyer, Samuel
1858-1940

Samuel Untermyer was a counsel of The House Banking Committee. He testified about the inside information that many corporate leaders had concerning their own companies, but failed to make public. Usually, they used the information to trade in their own stock or the stock of companies in which they were outside directors.

Untermyer made a prophetic statement before the committee. "It will not be long before corporate officers will be prevented from withholding information and speculating on advance knowledge. The time will come when these members of The New York Stock Exchange who are bitterly assailing and slandering the champions of this legislation will find that it has marked the dawn of a new era of usefulness for them and the exchange."

Untermyer was perfectly correct, but the day was still twenty years away. It took the stock market crash and the great depression before legislation was passed to prevent insider trading abuses and the lack of uniform reporting.

Vanderbilt, Cornelius
1794-1877

Cornelius Vanderbilt is one of the most dominant figures in America's financial history. He was born of poor Dutch peasants in 1794. His career spanned the flight of time and the changes that developed from steamships, railroads, the telegraph, and the steel industry.

The California gold rush brought his 100 steamships profits of $100,000 each month. By 1853, he had a fortune of $11,000,000, which he kept at 25 percent. Vanderbilt was fabulously rich, but he kept his complex ventures in his head. He trusted no one. His own son, William H. Vanderbilt knew nothing of his father's methods. Commodore Vanderbilt had nine children. He never competed with his opposition. He wrote them,

"Gentlemen, you have undertaken to cheat me. I will not sue you, for law takes too long. I will ruin you." And he did.

Cornelius Vanderbilt was one of the first captains of industry. He was no pioneer, but entered an industry when it was in a fruitful stage. He drove himself with a reckless energy. In the Harlem Corner he could have destroyed the whole financial community. Such was his awesome power. Daniel Drew was short and was forced to pay half a million as the price was driven up to $179 dollars a share. Vanderbilt said, "put it up to a thousand!" But he agreed to settle for $285 a share.

There was a fight for Erie and Vanderbilt tried to corner the stock. Drew had Jim Fisk and Jay Gould to help him. By 1866, Vanderbilt had bought enough Erie to claim that he was adding it to his growing system. But "The Erie Ring" kept issuing more stock, and sent Erie down from 95 to 50. Drew, Fisk, and Gould authorized a new convertible bond issue ($10 million). The Commodore continued to buy "every damn share that's offered." Judge George C. Barnard of The New York Supreme Court (William Tweed Ring) ordered a return to the treasury of one quarter of the shares issued and $3 million of the convertible bonds. Erie then rose 30 points to 84. It looked like the bears were cornered at last. Vanderbilt had 200,000 shares.

Jay Gould emerged as a leader and displayed a crafty boldness which was worthy of a foe of Vanderbilt. He found a judge of the state's Supreme Court who issued a counter injunction and "The Erie Ring" took the whole $10 million of newly issued bonds and converted them into 100,000 shares of stock. It was Vanderbilt against the printing press. Judge Barnard ordered "The Ring" arrested. They fled to New Jersey on March 11, 1868. Jay Gould slipped into Albany with a valise full of money and succeeded in buying the necessary votes to have "The Erie Bill of 1868" passed in his favor. The bill approved the bond issue. He had beaten the Commodore. Gould posed as the savior of the people who would be at Vanderbilt's mercy if he controlled both The New York Central and The Erie. Vanderbilt sent a message to Drew later in 1868. "I'm sick of the whole damned business. Come and see me." The meeting resulted in a truce and included a return of some money to the Commodore.

"The Erie Ring" returned to New York City in triumph. Drew was ousted by Gould in a brilliant corner. Drew was ruined. Gould was called, "The Mephistopheles of Wall Street."

Vanderbilt fell sick in 1876, and on January 4, 1877 he passed away. He left the bulk of his estate of $94,000,000 dollars in securities to his son, William Henry Vanderbilt. It was regarded as the first industrial fortune in the world.

In his last years Vanderbilt consulted spirit mediums, played whist, switched from gin to beer, chased the female servants in his home, and married a twenty-nine year old distant cousin. He did build New York City's Grand Central Terminal.

Vanderbilt, William Henry
1821-1885

William H. Vanderbilt was relegated to living on a farm until he was forty-five. His father thought he was sluggish and stupid. William H. Vanderbilt eventually won the confidence of his father. He was prone to compromise rather than fight.

William prospered and in eight years he doubled the fortune his father had taken ten times as long to accumulate. For all his successes during his life he will be remembered for his famous quote, "the public be damned!" In reality, he followed up these words with, "I am working for my stockholders, if the public want the train why don't they pay for it?"

His monopoly of a section of the country sustained him well, and he died suddenly in 1885. His affairs were undergoing a significant change. His estate of $100,000,000 was diversified into hundreds of enterprises which were enough to provide for his many heirs.

Vassar, Matthew
1792-1868

Matthew Vassar was an English-born American brewer and merchant. He founded Vassar College in 1861. He was born in Norfolk, England. He immigrated to New York with his family in 1796. His parents had him apprenticed to a tanner when he was 14.

He ran away to Newburgh, New York and entered the brewing business. At the age of 18 he took over his family's brewery and he developed his Poughkeepsie's brewery into one of the largest in the country. He made a sizable personal fortune in the process.

He established a woman's college in Poughkeepsie. He presented The Board of Trustees with a tin box containing half of his fortune ($408,000 or $ 9,700,000 in 2008 dollars). He also gave them the deed for 200 acres of land to establish a campus. On June 23, 1868, Vassar delivered his farewell address to the Vassar College Board of Trustees. He died in the middle of delivering the eleventh page of the speech.

Villard, Henry (Heinrich Hilgard)
1835-1900

German-born Henry Villard had started a newspaper career as a youth. He came west for Horace Greeley's Tribune, and bought The Columbia River Line for much less than its real value. He then accumulated Northern Pacific and pushed through its completion.

He drove "The Golden Spike" in 1883, but the road had a deficit of $55 million and construction costs exceeded estimates by $14 million. In a few months, Villard stepped down and his company quietly went bankrupt. Nevertheless, Villard attracted thousands of immigrants who bought land and built up the Northwest Territory.

Villard was a Bavarian who came to the United States in 1853 and proceeded to Colorado. He was a journalist for a German language paper and a war correspondent for Horace Greeley's Tribune. He also worked for Jay Cooke. He was quick-witted, magnetic, and eloquent. He attracted friends everywhere. In 1871 he revisited Bavaria and returned in 1874 as financial agent for defrauded German bondholders. Villard was dazzled by the beautiful frontier, giant forests, minerals, rich farmlands in the Oregon valleys. At that time the western limit of the Northern Pacific was at Bismarck, North Dakota on the Missouri River.

Villard in a coup was able to gain control of the Oregon Railway and Navigation Company, soon valued at $10 million with a $100,000 option, a mortgage, and bond sales. The price rose to 95 in Wall Street due to a large dividend (8%) and great earnings. Woerishoffer bulled the stock to 200. Villard seized the mountain passes and valleys. In 1880 he foiled a secret attempt to raise $40 million to complete and equip the Northern Pacific. He formed a syndicate and bought control in the open market. Villard's new holding company, The Oregon & Transcontinental Company with his aggressive agents inspired 6,000 wagon trains to cross the Rockies, with Germans, Scandinavians, and Russians. In the end, Villard was overextended in debt and his Oregon & Transcontinental collapsed in 1884. He resigned in disgrace. The hero had become the butt of public anger.

Walgreen, Charles
1873-1939

Born in Knoxville, Illinois, Charles Walgreen was the son of Swedish immigrants. He worked for a pharmacist in Dixon, Illinois and went to Chicago and became a licensed pharmacist (1893). He was in the Cavalry during the Spanish-American War

Walgreen returned to Chicago after the war and bought the store from Isaac Blood. By 1916, he owned nine drug stores. By 1927, he had 110 stores. While serving in Cuba he contracted Yellow Fever, which plagued him for the rest of his life.

Walgreen's son and grandson continued to play dominant roles in the company. Charles Walgreen Jr. died at 110 years of age. There were 5,500 Walgreen stores in 47 states and 500 were scheduled to open in 2007.

Walton, Sam Moore
1918-1992

Sam Walton was the founder of one of the most successful businesses in American history. The year before his death in 1992, the Walton fortune was more than $22 billion. He divided his estate to his wife and four children. If the fortune had remained in the hands of one person, it would have easily overshadowed those of Warren Buffett and Bill Gates.

Sam Walton was a natural salesman. He was born in Oklahoma and grew up in Columbia, Missouri. When he graduated from the University of Missouri he went to work for J.C. Penney. In 1942 Walton served with the military police stateside. He operated his own variety store in Newport, Arkansas, part of a national chain of Ben Franklin Stores. He built a chain of sixteen Ben Franklin Stores. Then Sam Walton opened his own discount store in Rogers, Arkansas. The secret of Walton's success was to focus on small towns and building central warehouses arranged around them like the spokes of a wheel. All the stores were within one day by truck from the warehouse.

Within eight years Walton opened thirty stores. In 1970 he took the company public. Success never changed Sam Walton. When it was announced that he was America's richest man he was driving around Bentonville in an old pick-up truck and having his hair cut in the local barber shop. The three most important things were "the customer, the customer, and the customer." Sam Walton died of bone cancer in 1992.

Wanamaker, John
1838-1922

John Wanamaker was the most innovative and flamboyant department store owner in America. He adopted the policy of one-price and followed it with a guarantee of satisfaction or money refund. Wanamaker proclaimed these virtues so loudly and persistently that they came to be identified with his store more than any other.

He opened a men's and boy's store in 1861 with his brother-in-law Nathan Brown in Philadelphia. It says a great deal about Wanamaker that of the $2,467 in receipts from the first day's business, he invested $24 in advertising. The ads never stopped. Brown died in 1868, and Wanamaker bought out his interest from his estate.

In the early 1870s, with business booming, John Wanamaker opened branch stores in Pittsburgh, Memphis, St. Louis, Baltimore, Richmond, and Louisville, but sold them to their managers. He bought the old Pennsylvania rail freight depot, and stocked it with $500,000 worth of merchandise. The next year he moved into the refurbished hall, which he called the Wanamaker Grand Depot. The opening was so well advertised that 70,000 people swarmed into the store on the first day.

Warburg, Felix
1871-1937

Felix Warburg was the handsomest man in town. Frieda Schiff, daughter of Jacob Schiff, the strong leader of Kuhn, Loeb & Co. was told that she must meet Felix Warburg. The Warburg's were from Hamburg. The family bank, M.M. Warburg & Company was founded in 1798, and it lasted until the Hitler era, when it was confiscated.

Felix loved beautiful women, music, books, paintings, horses, etc. He was a rebel. He scorned the orthodoxy of his parents. Felix went to a party given by the Dreyfus's. He met Frieda Schiff there, and when he went home he knocked on his parents' door and said, "I have met the girl I'm going to marry."

Felix did marry Frieda, and this automatically brought him into Kuhn, Loeb. He left Germany and he arrived in New York in 1895, and immediately went to work

Warburg, Paul
1868-1932

Paul Warburg, a member of the German-American Banking House and a member of one of New York's prominent banking families, was one of the architects of the principles creating The Federal Reserve System.

The Aldrich Plan outlined the blueprint for the newly created Federal Reserve in 1913. Nelson Aldrich was a Republican Senator from Rhode Island. Warburg was offered the job as Chairman of the Fed, but he turned it down. He did serve as a Director until 1918.

Ward, Montgomery Aaron
1843-1913

Montgomery Ward was founded by Aaron Montgomery Ward in 1872. He astutely reasoned that rural customers could buy goods by mail and pick them up at the nearest train station.

After recovering from the Great Chicago Fire, Ward started his business in a single room. He had two partners and $1,800 in capital. The first catalogue in 1872 consisted of a single sheet. By 1883, the book had grown to 240 pages. Serious competition appeared in 1900 when Richard Sears entered the mail-order business. Ward's had sales of $8.7 million, Sears had $10 million.

By 1904, 3 million catalogues were mailed to customers. Ward died in 1913 after 41 years in the business. Ward's opened 244 stores. By 1929 it had 531 stores. In 1930 it turned down a merger offer from Sears. In 1939, Sewell Avery was hired as President.

After World War II, sales declined, but Montgomery Ward was still the 3rd largest department store chain. After a nationwide strike President Roosevelt ordered all Montgomery Ward property seized. President Truman ended the seizure and the Supreme Court ended the pending appeal as moot.

Washington, George
1732-1799

The father of our country had an estate of $500,000 at the time of his death. George Washington did not accept pay as Commander-in-Chief during The Revolutionary War. He turned down $500 per month salary. He only asked for his expenses. In fact, he offered to finance an Army to fight England.

Washington was a surveyor, and built his wealth by accumulating land and marrying a wealthy widow, Martha Curtis. He owned land in Virginia, Maryland, Pennsylvania, New York, Kentucky, and other places. By the age of 28 he owned nearly 1,500 acres. Martha Curtis' first husband left her a 17,000 acre estate worth $360,000.

When Washington died in 1799 at the age of sixty-seven, he left his estate to Martha and his slaves, with the instruction that they should be set free after her death.

Watson, Thomas John Sr.
1874-1956

Thomas Watson was undoubtedly one of the greatest salesmen of his time. He directed the growth of International Business Machines from 1914 to 1956, and it developed into an international force that made him one of the world's richest men.

He worked on his father's farm in upstate New York, and then his father started a lumber business in Painted Post, New York. After a brief period of working as a salesman for $10 a week, Watson moved to Buffalo. He opened a butcher shop, which soon failed, leaving Watson with no money and no job.

Watson had a cash register in the butcher shop for which he had to arrange for installment payments. He visited NCR and asked for a job. It wasn't easy, but he finally was hired in 1896. John Range taught Watson how to be a successful salesman and he became the best salesman in the East, earning $100 a week.

It wasn't long before Watson was called to NCR's main office in Dayton, Ohio. In 1914 Watson was hired as general manager of the Computing Tabulating Recording Company. Within 4 years Watson became President and doubled its revenues to $9 million dollars. In 1924, he renamed the company, International Business Machines. By 1952, Watson built IBM into such a dominant company that more than 90 percent of all tabulating machines in the United States were owned or leased to its customers. When Watson died in 1956, IBM's revenues were $897 million, and the company had 72,500 employees.

Weightman, William
1813-1904

William Weightman founded one of the first U.S. pharmaceutical firms, and made his fortune producing sugar-coated Quinine pills. His real estate investments in Philadelphia also made him wealthy.

Born in England, he came to the U.S. to work for his uncle at the age of sixteen. His uncle owned a chemical manufacturing company. As a boy Weightman worked in the laboratory and became a brilliant chemist.

Weightman's firm became one of the international leaders in chemical manufacturing and pharmaceuticals. After his death, the company he founded joined with another firm and was then absorbed by Merck & Company in 1927.

Weightman invested in theaters, hotels, office buildings, and businesses and residential blocks in the heart of Philadelphia. His chemical business and his real estate investments made him the richest man in Pennsylvania.

Weightman left nearly his entire $80 million fortune to his daughter, and after winning the right to keep her fortune, and defeating those who contested the will, Ann Walker lived in regal fashion in New York, with homes in Atlantic City and the Philadelphia suburbs.

Weill, Sanford I. (Sandy)
1933-

Sanford Weill was born and raised in Brooklyn, New York. After he graduated from Cornell University in 1955, he married his wife Joan. He started working as a $35 a week runner for Bear Stearns. He soon became a broker, and while still in his twenties he opened a small brokerage company, "Carter, Berlind, Potoma, and Weill.

Twenty years and fifteen acquisitions later, Weill was leading Shearson, the second largest company in the business. He sold Shearson to American Express for $930 million. Weill became President of American Express, but he resigned in 1985.

At 53, Weill took over as CEO of Commercial Credit. He acquired Primerica for $1.5 billion. He now owned Smith, Barney & Co. and an insurance company, A.L. Williams. His next move was the purchase of 27 percent of Traveler's Insurance for $733.5 million. That year he earned $67.6 million. He then repurchased Shearson from American Express for $1.2 billion. Shearson then merged with Smith, Barney. Shearson had 8,400 brokers. Weill then acquired the remaining shares of Traveler's for $4 billion in stock. In 1996, he bought the Property and Casualty business of Aetna for $4 billion.

In September 1997, Traveler's paid $9.1 billion to buy Salomon, Inc., parent of Salomon Brothers. Then in 1998, Weill merged Traveler's with Citicorp. After reaching the zenith of his career, Co-Chairman and Co-CEO of Citigroup, with $13 billion in earnings in 2001, Weill retired in 2003 and 2006 from Chairman and CEO of Citigroup.

Today, Sanford and Joan live in Greenwich, Connecticut. The Weill's have contributed generously to Carnegie Hall, Cornell University, Weill-Cornell Medical College, and the University of Michigan. Sanford and Joan Weill personally contributed $250 million.

Wells, Henry
1805-1878

In addition to organizing Wells, Fargo & Company with William G. Fargo in 1852, Henry Wells co-founded The American Express Company in 1850 and served as President for its first 18 years. He also founded Wells College for Women in Aurora, New York in 1868.

Both Henry Wells and William G. Fargo began their careers as express men in upstate New York. They joined forces with other express operators in 1845 to extend their business to Chicago and St. Louis, the Western edge of what was then The United States.

This was a formative period for the express industry with companies forming, dissolving, and consolidating. One such merger led to the creation of The American Express Company in 1850, with Wells as President and Fargo as Secretary. Business was plentiful for the company, with the assurance of a reliable railway transportation system being built throughout the East.

Gold was discovered in California in 1849 and Congress granted statehood to California in 1850. On March 18, 1852, Wells, Fargo & Co. was born.

Westinghouse, George Jr.
1846-1914

George Westinghouse, a New York engineer, became wealthy developing a railroad air brake. The device required a pulsating current, known as alternating current. Thomas Edison was opposed to it, and preferred direct current. He believed alternating current can kill people.

Westinghouse won "the war of the currents." By 1900, $1 billion was invested in the business of electric lighting. American electrical equipment makers sold more than $5 million worth of their products abroad. It was mostly alternating current, not direct current. General Electric, the industrial giant that grew out of Edison's pioneering work was making most of its products to be powered by alternating current.

Weyerhaeuser, Frederick
1834-1914

Frederick Weyerhaeuser was born in Germany and came to the United States when he was twenty. "Dutch Fred" took a job in a lumber company and was promoted to foreman. He then bought a lumber yard at auction, and with his brother-in-law gained control of a second mill.

Fred's neighbor in St. Paul was James J. Hill the railroad man. While building the Northern Pacific Railway, Hill was given enormous land grants between The Rockies and The Cascades. Hill had no use for the land and Weyerhaeuser had an idea for those verdant forests. He and his associates bought 900,000 acres for $6 a share. Thus, he locked up the last great timber lands in the United States. The Weyerhaeuser family controlled 62,500 square miles, an area the size of Wisconsin. They also had interests in twenty sawmills.

Weyerhaeuser had four sons and after he died in 1914, his eldest son John took over. His son John Jr. graduated from Yale and succeeded his father. His eldest son George succeeded him.

The Weyerhaeuser Corporation controlled 5.8 million acres of forest land. It had 48,000 employees and had sales in 1978 of $44 billion. In the 1980s the company lost its leadership to the Georgia-Pacific Corporation.

Whitney, Eli
1765-1825

Eli Whitney was a Yale graduate who went south as a tutor. He became aware of the need to remove the seeds from the short-staple cotton. Within ten days he built a model of the machine that was needed. It was promptly stolen before Whitney was able to get a patent. However, he did get a patent with Miller who supplied the capital for the new enterprise. The firm went broke, and Whitney and Miller gave up the cotton gin business.

The cotton gin developed the spectacular growth of cotton from 2 million pounds in 1790 to 80 million pounds in 1815. Eventually Miller and Whitney were able to have a small share of the new cotton wealth.

In 1798, Eli Whitney contacted Oliver Wolcott, Secretary of the Treasury, and offered to manufacture ten to fifteen thousand arms. He was awarded a contract to produce 10,000 muskets at $13.40 each. He received a $5,000 advance.

.

Widener, Peter Arrell Brown
1834-1915

Peter Arrell Widener built the largest transit empire in the nation and became the richest man in Philadelphia. His father was a bricklayer. He dropped out of high school and worked in a meat market. He was in his own business very soon and became an important figure in the city's Republican Party. During the Civil War Widener received a contract to supply mutton for Union troops, earning him $50,000. Widener then used the earnings from his chain of meat stores to buy up the street railways of Philadelphia.

By 1895, Widener's expanded business could carry more than 100 million passengers. He also worked with Thomas Fortune Ryan and William Collins Whitney to dominate New York Transit. Widener and partners moved to invest in rail systems in Chicago, Pittsburgh, and Baltimore. They eventually owned streetcar tracks with a total capitalization of about $1.5 billion.

Widener invested in U.S. Steel, American Tobacco, and Standard Oil, as well as railroads and mortgage companies. Widener had three sons, and the only surviving son, George D. Widener took over his father's transit interests. When the elder Widener died he was eighty-one, and he was the richest man in Philadelphia. He left a fortune of $100 million.

Woolworth, Frank Winfield
1852-1919

Frank W. Woolworth grew up on a farm in Great Bend, New York. After working as a clerk in a store for $3.50 a week, he worked his way up to $6.00 a week. He got a job in Michigan for $10 a week in a 99 cent store. It was enough for him to get married. Woolworth was a failure as a salesman, and he came close to taking his life. He spent a year on his father's farm.

His old employer rehired him at $10 a week. Woolworth was good at setting up stores and dressing shop windows. He set up a store in Utica, New York with 5 cent items. It proved to be a failure. Undaunted by his failures Woolworth opened a store in Lancaster, Pennsylvania and added a 10 cent line to the 5 cent line. It was just the margin needed for success. The 5 and 10 cent store model covered the nation.

Woolworth's first store was opened in 1879. Fifteen years later he had 28 stores with sales of more than $1 million. By 1912, Woolworth's stores under his name and other chains had grown to nearly 600 stores, and had $65 million in sales. It was the largest merchandising firm in America. In 1913, Woolworth built the building that bears his name, the tallest building in New York City.

At his death in 1919, he owned more than one thousand stores in North America, selling more than $100 million in goods per year. He had built a fortune of more than $65 million.

Wright Brothers
Orville   1867-1948
Wilbur   1867-1912

On a sandy beach at Kitty Hawk, North Carolina, Orville Wright flew a powered, heavier-than-air machine for twelve seconds, and his brother Wilbur first repeated the feat and then piloted their primitive airplane 852 feet in fifty-nine seconds, before landing safely.

The Wrights, who were bicycle mechanics, became interested in flying during the 1890s. Their achievements attracted more attention abroad than in their own country. They organized a company in France, and built a plane that could sustain flight for an hour at a speed of forty miles an hour, landing undamaged, and that could carry two men and adequate fuel to fly 125 miles.

Wrigley, William Jr.
1861-1932

William Wrigley worked in his father's soap factory. At twenty-nine he established a business in Chicago. They made soap and baking powder. He found that customers wanted chewing gum. He immediately changed the business.

Wrigley developed "Wrigley's Spearmint gum" in 1893. By 1910 it was the top-selling gum in America. Before his death in 1932 he was selling $75 million worth of gum per year. Wrigley bought the Chicago Cubs

At his death, the value of his holdings was estimated at $34 million. The family holds 35 percent of the stock. In 1983 it was worth $300 million. In 1985, Forbes held the Wrigley family fortune at $15 billion.

Wynn, Steve (Stephen Alan)
1942-

Steve Wynn was born in New Haven, Connecticut, Stephen Alan Weinberg. Steve was raised in Utica, New York. He studied English Literature at the University of Pennsylvania. He graduated with a Bachelor of Arts degree. His father died in 1963, leaving gaming debts of $350,000. He was running a group of bingo parlors and Wynn took over the operation in Maryland.

His success led to an investment in the Frontier Hotel and casino in Las Vegas. He and his wife Elaine moved to Las Vegas in 1967. Steve owned a wine and liquor importing company from 1968 to 1972. Profits from a land deal involving Howard Hughes and Caesar's Palace led Wynn into a controlling interest in the Golden Nugget, Las Vegas. He also owned the Golden Nugget in Atlantic City.

His first major strip casino was The Mirage, which opened in 1989. The $630 million cost was financed by junk bonds issued by Michael Milken. It became extremely lucrative and made Wynn a major factor in Las Vegas' success. In 1991 Golden Nugget, Inc. was named Mirage Resorts, Inc. Treasure Island opened in 1993 at a cost of $450 million. In 1998, the more opulent Bellagio was opened at a cost of $1.6 billion. It was the most expensive hotel in the world. The Bellagio started a spree of luxurious developments including The Venetian, Mandalay Bay, and Paris Las Vegas.

In 1999 Wynn built the 1,835 room Beau Rivage in Biloxi, Mississippi. In June 2000, Mirage Resorts was sold to MGM Grand, Inc. for $6.6 billion. Five weeks earlier, Wynn bought The Desert Inn for $270 million. He sold it in 18 weeks and took Wynn Resorts Ltd. Public in 2002. In 2005, Steve Wynn built The Wynn, Las Vegas on the site of The Desert Inn

The Wynn Macao opened in 2006. In the summer of 2008, Wynn started hiring 3,500 employees for The Encore. The Wynn Encore Macao was opened in 2010.

Zeckendorf, William
1905-1976

William Zeckendorf was a prominent real estate developer. He started working for Webb and Knapp in 1938. He bought the company in 1949. He developed the New York urban landscape. His acquisition of a 17 acre site between 42nd Street and 48th Street on the East River was bought by Nelson Rockefeller's father, John D. Rockefeller Jr. It was subsequently donated for the building of the United Nations Headquarters.

Zeckendorf owned the Chrysler Building, the Hotel Astor, and he built the Mile High Center in Denver, Colorado, and The Place Ville Marie in Montreal, Canada. In 1958 he made a deal with Spyros Skouras, Head of Twentieth Century Fox to develop 176 acres in Los Angeles into a proposed $400 million Century City. It took a joint-venture relationship with Alcoa to finally build Century City, which grew to a $500 million project.

Before the bankruptcy of the company in 1965, Zeckendorf developed Roosevelt Airfield, where Charles Lindbergh began his transatlantic flight, and Long Island University. Zeckendorf used his deal-making skills to acquire and build projects for which he lacked the funds, but in time, the under-funding caught up with him.

Zuckerberg, Mark
1984-

The meteoric career of Mark Zuckerberg is unprecedented in the history of business. Today, Facebook has close to one billion active users. It is a social platform that has taken the internet to stunning success and has been the subject of a blockbuster Hollywood movie.

Zuckerberg and his co-founders launched Facebook from his Harvard University dorm room. His father, Edward, is a dentist who taught Mark programming. He used computers and wrote software in middle school. He was a prodigy and a crack programmer who was wooed by Microsoft when he was in Phillips Exeter Academy. Instead, he went to Harvard.

At the age of nineteen Zuckerberg built an application for Harvard's 6,000 students to stay connected with their friends and family. It took only "a couple of weeks." One month later, Facebook expanded to Columbia, Stanford, and Yale. Zuckerberg and his friends moved to Palo Alto, California for the summer. But Silicon Valley took hold and they stayed. By the end of the first year Facebook had nearly one million users. Funding of $12.7 million from Accel Partners in 2005 allowed Facebook to expand to more than 800 colleges.

Building a company was Zuckerberg's choice so he never went back to Harvard. There were 5 million users of Facebook. Today, there are over 750,000,000 users all over the world and Facebook is now a public company.

Zukor, Adolph
1873-1976

Adolph was a Hungarian film mogul, and founder of Paramount Pictures. Zukor was born in Riese, Hungary in 1873. When he was 16, in 1889, he immigrated to the United States. He landed in New York. He worked in an upholstery shop. He then got a job as an apprentice at a furrier.

In 1893 The Columbian Exposition drew him to Chicago where he started a fur company. In the second year he had expanded to twenty-five employees, and he opened a branch.

Zukor was a wealthy young man who had an apartment in the fashionable section of New York, (11th Street and Seventh Avenue). In 1918 he moved to New City. He bought 300 acres from Lawrence Abraham, heir to A & S Department Stores. Two years later he bought 500 more acres. He built a golf course, guest house, a movie theater, and staff quarters. Today, the Zukor Estate is a private country club known as the Paramount Country Club.

In 1903 his cousin Max Goldstein asked for a loan to expand his chain of theaters. Zukor gave Max the loan and formed a partnership to open another theater. Another partner was Marcus Loew.

Zukor went on to form Famous Players-Lasky with Jesse Lasky. He then founded Paramount Pictures. He was a director and a producer. He was president until 1936. In 1959 he was elevated to Chairman Emeritus, a position which he held until his death at the age of 103.

Bibliography

Aaseng, Nathan
    Business Builders in Fast Food
2001   Oliver Press, Inc.

Achievement, Academy of

Baruch, Bernard M.
    Baruch: My Own Story
1957   Henry Holt and Company

Birmingham, Stephen
    Our Crowd
1967   Harper & Row Publishers

Brooks, John
    The Go Go Years
1973   Weybright and Talley

Byrne, John A.
    World Changers—Entrepreneurs who Changed
Business as we Know it
2011

Chamberlain, John
    The Enterprising Americans
1974   Harper & Row Publishers

Ellis, Charles D. with James R. Vertin

Wall Street People—Volume 2
2003   John Wiley & Sons, Inc.

Ferry, John William
    History of the Department Store
1960   The MacMillan Company

Fisher, Kenneth L.
    100 Minds That Made the Market
1993   Business Classics

Forbes

Fowler, William Worthington
    Twenty Years in Wall Street
1880   Orange Judd Co.

Geisst, Charles R.
    Wall Street—A History From its Beginnings to the Fall
of Enron
2004   Oxford University Press

Google

Groner, Alex
    American Business and Industry
1972   American Heritage Publishing Co., Inc.

Josephson, Matthew
    The Robber Barons
1934   Harcourt Brace & World Inc.

Klepper, Michael and Robert Gunther
    The Wealthy 100
1996   Citadel Press—Carol Publishing Group

Lundberg, Ferdinand
    The Rich and Super Rich
1968   Lyle Stuart, Inc.

MacKay Charles
    Extraordinary Popular Delusions and the Madness of
Crowds
1841   Richard Bentley   1932   L.C. Page & Co.

Medberry, James F.
    Men and Mysteries of Wall Street
1870   Field, Osgood & Co.
Retail Hall of Fame

Schultz, Harry D. and Samson H. Coslow
    A Treasury of Wall Street Wisdom
1966   Investor's Press

Sobel, Robert
    The Curbstone Brokers
1970   The MacMillan Company
    The Entrepreneurs
1974   Weybright and Talley

Tebbel, John
    The Inheritors

1962   G.P. Putnam's Sons

Thiers, Adolphe
   John Law and the Mississippi Bubble
1859   W.A. Townsend   1868   Greenwood Press

Wikipedia

Wyckoff, Richard D.
   Wall Street Ventures and Adventures
1930   Harper & Row Publishers

Zerden, Sheldon
   Best Books on the Stock Market
1972   R.R.Bowker Company (Xerox)

About the Author

Sheldon Zerden was an investment advisor and portfolio manager with Prudential Securities for forty years. He was the financial editor for several newspapers including The Market Chronicle, The Brooklyn Times, and The Soho Weekly News.

Zerden published a major work which contained analytical reviews of 150 of the best books on Wall Street. It was titled, "Best Books on the Stock Market : An Analytical Bibliography.
It was selected as the best book in finance by the American Library Association.

Following that award-winning book, Zerden wrote "Margin Power": an aggressive strategy for making a fortune in the stock market.

His interest in health has led to several books in the area of healthcare. The latest work is "The Best of Health: The 100 Best Health Books."

Author's Note

The substantial bibliography that was used to create "The Wall Street Hall of Fame" was essential to develop the personality profiles of its members.

My award-winning book, "Best Books on the Stock Market" was helpful in defining the contributions of the Hall of Fame. This book had to be written. It is a veritable history of American business as seen through the lives of the great people who helped build our country into the greatest economic power in the world.

The biographical portraits of the members of "The Wall Street Hall of Fame" have been obtained from sources that are believed to be reliable.